THE MUSEUM OF
THE HUNGARIAN VILLAGE
AT SZENTENDRE

Title of the Hungarian original: Szabadtéri Néprajzi Múzeum
Szentendrén, Corvina Kiadó, Budapest, 1989.

On the front cover: Streetscape of the group of buildings from the
Plain in North-Western Hungary

On the back cover: Chimneyless kitchen with an open hearth in
Szentgyörgyvölgy (Photo by Péter Deim)

Translated by Inez Kemenes
Translation revised by Alexander Fenton

Figures by Tibor Sabján, András Szalai, Mrs. Sándor Lázár,
Klára K. Csilléry and Gábor Suppan

Design by János Lengyel

ISBN 963 13 2895 3

Printed in Hungary, 1990
Kossuth Printing House
CO 2813–h–9094

THE MUSEUM OF THE HUNGARIAN VILLAGE AT SZENTENDRE

A Guided Tour Around the Open Air Ethnographic
Museum of Szentendre

EDITED BY PÉTER KECSKÉS

CORVINA

CONTENTS

INTRODUCTION

The background to the appearance of a new type of museum, the open air museum with its accompanying ethnographic collections, lies in the last third of the 19th century, when special exhibitions were mounted in more than one European country. One of the guiding principles of the organizers of these world exhibitions (e.g. Paris, 1867; Vienna, 1873) was the recognition that there was a historical connection between folklore and national culture. They aimed to illustrate this interaction as clearly as possible by moving away from the traditional form of museum collection and towards living collections of houses and articles of furniture in their natural environment. The idea of transferring such items worthy of preservation and presentation into one place, arranged like a park, was first put into practice in Stockholm, in 1891.

These world exhibitions also taught another lesson. In line with upper class principles of social reform, it was considered that the display of houses of popular character, or having the characteristic features of small regions, could point the way to inexpensive and practical housing for the "oppressed working classes".

The purchase of "ancient", "original" and "homecraft" items was seen as a way of resisting the unifying effect on the furniture and "inhumanly uniform, soulless" products of industrialization.

In an age of national awakening, such endeavours appeared not only in Western Europe and Scandinavia but also in parts of Central Europe (Lemberg [now Lvov] 1894; Prague 1895). A century later, under different historical, but similar social circumstances, the need for developing national open air collections once more emerged in East-Central Europe.

In 1896 the Budapest Millenary Exhibition (in celebration of the conquest of the country one thousand years earlier by the ancestors of the Hungarians) demonstrated both the history of the nation and presented furnished peasant houses made by local craftsmen. These houses were judged as representative of Hungarian culture by the ethnographer János Jankó (1868–1902). Mirroring the proportions shown by contemporary population statistics, half of the houses (12) came from territories inhabited by Hungarians, whereas the other half represented the folk architecture of various minorities. Although previous research was based on the concept of "one nationality, one architectural character", János Jankó was able to demonstrate that by the end of the 19th century the house of room–kitchen–pantry arrangement had become universal throughout the Carpathian Basin. He also documented the heating devices of kitchens and rooms and the utilization of household objects. Regrettably the Ethnographic Village of the Millenary Exhibition was dismantled in 1897. Besides documents, only a few of the objects from it remain today in the Budapest Ethnographical Museum, founded in 1872.

The idea of founding "a true ethnographic or national museum" received little attention even after Zsigmond Bátky (1874–1939) urged in 1906 the setting up of "a folk museum containing complete peasant farms, with everything living in them, to be set up in the open air". Along with Károly Viski (1882–1945) and László Vargha (1904–84), it was István Györffy (1884–1939) who published the plan in 1938 for a Skanzen (or open-air museum on the lines of the one set up at Skanzen in Sweden) to be erected in the Budapest public gardens (Népliget) as part of a comprehensive programme for national education. (The word Skanzen was by that time already a common word in the Hungarian language.)

However, the economic and cultural-political conditions between the two world wars were not favourable for the establishment of a central open air ethnographic collection. Apart from György Domanovszky's (1909–1984) plan published in 1940, ideas for regional projects (Vasi, Tihany, Nagykun Skanzen) began to appear. Some rural peasant houses had already been preserved in situ, but folk architecture had not yet fallen under the protective wing of historic monuments.

In 1959 the Ethnographic Committee of the Hungarian Academy of Sciences and the Ethnographical Museum called a conference to discuss the possibilities for bringing a national open air collection into existence. Gyula Ortutay (1910–78) stressed that when undertaking this task the points of view of ethnography, architecture, the protection of monuments and foreign tourist traffic had to be considered carefully.

The possibility of establishing the Szentendre Open Air Ethnographic Museum within the framework of the Budapest Ethnographical Museum, was opened up in 1965 as part of a cultural-political resolution. By April 1967, four people, and by 1969 a team of twelve museologists, mostly ethnographers, were working on a scientific method of selecting buildings, making plans for dismantling, re-building, preserving, maintaining and furnishing them. The Village Museum became an independent institution with a national collecting remit on 1st of January, 1972, and has been operating in Szentendre since August, 1974. It occupies 46 hectares lying 5 kilometres north-west of the town.

The scientific and technical plans of the Museum are based on the results of researches into ethnography and the history of settlements, architecture and techniques, carried out by three generations of ethnographers. The importance of all their research work, done expressly in the interests of creating this Museum, work revealing local patterns of exterior and interior decoration, building variations, ways of life and the connections between economy, society and education, has been vital. In fact the Village Museum of Szentendre is a central undertaking of this branch of science comparable to the *Magyar Néprajzi Lexikon* (The Ethnographical Encyclopaedia of Hungary), the *Magyar Néprajzi Atlasz* (The Atlas of Hungarian Ethnography) or the series of volumes detailing the ethnography of the Hungarian race. It differs only in the method and form of realization, though in many respects it is more complicated and expensive. At such a permanent exhibition the historical value, type and authenticity of the building, "the installation" are just as important as the contents reflecting a way of life.

The collection spans ten distinct regional areas, the buildings representing typical versions and demonstrating the development which took place in the smaller and larger regions, villages and market towns from the middle of the 18th to the early years of the 20th century. The smallest museum unit is the croft, that is the plot where the farmhouse and farm buildings stand. Farm buildings in the fields (detached farmstead, barn, presshouse and cellar) are also shown, alongside communal buildings (church, belfry, cemetery, parish hall, etc.). The crofts and houses are arranged in the pattern of settlement characteristic of the region (e.g. a village made up of streets [utcás] or a spindle-shaped settlement [orsós] or the roadside village [útifalu], or the scatter of small nucleated units or hamlets, called szers) to the extent possible within the limits of what could be reconstructed within the museum. A regional unit usually consists of 4 to 8 crofts with the buildings orientated, if possible, as they were in their original place. The Village Museum's regional units are the Upper Tisza region, the Central Tisza region, a market town in the Great Hungarian Plain, Southern Transdanubia, Central Transdanubia, Western Transdanubia, the plain in Northwest Hungary (Little Plain), the northeast region of Hungary, Northern Hungary and a highland market town. It was not possible to transplant buildings that are no longer on Hungarian soil. However it was possible to refer to the culture of neighbouring territories (Csallóköz, Transylvania) as far as concerned certain types of construction, furniture and implements. The interior decoration of minorities living in Hungary is mainly represented in the groups of buildings from the plain in Northwest Hungary and the Great Hungarian Plain.

It should be noted that the constructions demonstrating a type are closely associated with the social level of their erection and development (cotter, feudal farmer, farmer, minor gentry, craftsman belonging to a guild, a peasant augmenting his income with some homecraft or their descendants). As part of the effort to make the Museum live there are "museum shows" to indicate means of production and consumption, the use of original utensils and general household life. According to family ability, time and opportunity for display you can see "reconstructions from the history of techniques" (hand-forging, grinding of wheat in a tread-mill, weaving hemp-cloth, baking bread, etc.). There is an increasing demand for such events; from the 1st of April to the end of October, while the museum is open, we have about a quarter of a million visitors.

The first regional unit to open for the public, that of the Upper Tisza region, was inaugurated in 1974. Since then five regional versions of this type of museum have come into being in Hungary: in Szombathely, Zalaegerszeg, Szenna, Ópusztaszer and Nyíregyháza.

Of the more than 320 buildings envisaged for the Village Museum, 82 had been made accessible to visitors by 1988 and another 120 are waiting for re-erection in the store-houses of the Museum. Unfortunately some have become unobtainable or had completely deteriorated and these will be replaced by other constructions, or exact copies will be prepared. Thus, roughly one third of the building project has been completed. The collection of museum articles is nearing 40,000 and there are in addition 70,000 photographs, 20,000 transparencies and 10,000 documentary items.

Of the ten planned regional units of the permanent exhibition, two have been completed to date. In the museum settlement representing the Upper Tisza region 2,700 objects can be seen in 32 buildings. The unit representing the plain in northeast Hungary comprises 42 constructions in which almost 7,000 objects can be studied. Construction work in the area allocated to West-ern Transdanubia (1,000 objects in 8 buildings) and the Great Hungarian Plain (tanner's house from Baja) has also begun.

Between 1969 and 1979 reconstructions and the collection of authentic buildings for museums were done by the Hungarian National Authority for Historical Monuments. Since then such tasks have been carried out by the Museum's own team of experts and skilled workers.

The Roman remains (Villa Rustica) found in the middle of the territory owned by the Museum brought new problems and new opportunities. This area had been allocated for the peasant crofts from the northern part of the Great Hungarian Plain. Due to the discovery the Museum had to apply for the expropriation of further land.

The Villa Rustica was the isolated farm of a legionary, discharged sometime in the 3rd or 4th century BC, who took up wine-growing and had one of the largest vineyards on the northern border of Pannonia. The building has been excavated, its better part preserved, and it is now "a museum within the museum".

The Village Museum has, since 1980, become a centre of scientific research enabling the organization of nation-wide research programmes, and their coordination with other teams working on related problems of social science. This is the centre for research into Hungarian vernacular architecture and interior decoration. The Archives of Hungarian Folk Architecture (A Magyar Népi Építészeti Archívum) have been established with a collection of original documents or copies, in order to create a national data bank. Through the arrangement of data from the geographical and thematic points of view it will be possible to evaluate work done till now and to set further realistic targets. With these activities a series entitled the Survey of Hungarian Folk Architecture (Magyar Népi Építészet Katasztere) will be published, in which the surveys of the relics of vernacular architecture will be published county by county. Another major task for the Museum is the classification of donated documents as they have to be handled separately. The Collection on Hungarian Vernacular Architecture is the bequest of László Vargha, a historian of architecture and an ethnographer. It consists of tens of thousands of photos, descriptions and surveys of buildings and furniture, valuable at a national level, most of which do not exist any more.

The fact that the tasks of the Museum include scientific preparatory work dismantling buildings, making plans for their re-erection and furnishing, preservation of material, rebuilding, maintenance and operation makes the staff ever keen to publish their latest findings. More unique information is becoming available as 18th and 19th century constructions are dismantled, especially if we consider that in the larger part of Hungary houses were not built of wood but of earth or clay. Research into the history and structure of incomplete or rebuilt buildings is very important, and the replicating of totally destroyed and irreplaceable houses on the basis of the data at our disposal is essential. Investigations uncover rare building structures and furnishings (upper cross embroidery, homespuns, earthenware, painted furniture) that can be identified on the basis of similar materials and techniques and whose preservation and reproduction is considered vital. These and similar questions are dealt with in the scientific and popular scientific publications of the Museum.

Our thanks are due to Corvina Press for enabling us to show the exhibits of our Museum, both re-erected and planned. Such information on the past two centuries of Hungarian villages and market towns will by tomorrow be part of our national cultural history.

In the Szentendre Village Museum, the Upper Tisza region was the first to be represented with a permanent exhibition opened in 1978 (Plate I).

The majority of the buildings and furnishings have come from the most archaic and, in respect of its material culture, most homogeneous part of the territory, from the villages of the Erdőhát, with additions from other parts of the Upper Tisza region, such as Tiszahát, Szamoshát, Túrhát or Bereg.

As a result of their peripheral position after the First World War, the Erdőhát villages have preserved their appearance, as shaped up to the turn of the century by their particular natural environment, their comparatively undisturbed development since the Middle Ages, their role as active mediators between the Great Hungarian Plain, the mountainous district and Transylvania, and their relationship with the minorities surrounding them. The traditional patterns of settlement, buildings and methods of construction, furniture and furnishings, farming implements, etc. have all been preserved and visitors to the museum can see the material environment of a way of life dating back in its essence to the age of feudalism.

The population that settled here between the 12th and 14th centuries made its dwelling places by the rivers, waters and moors, sometimes in spots that later became forest clearings. On elevations *(hátak)* that gave protection from floods (hence the names Erdőhát, Túrhát, Tiszahát, Szamoshát) tiny one-street villages came into being. In many instances the houses stood on one side of the street and the bank of the river or the rim of the bog formed the opposite side. The main street usually broadened out in the middle to give room for the church, a belfry and other public structures. Because of its layout, this type of settlement is sometimes called a "spindle village" *(orsós falu)*.

The region had economic contacts not with the Great Hungarian Plain which had similar geographical features, but with the hilly and mountainous regions (Sub-Carpathia, Szilágyság, Transylvania) where different methods of farming were in operation. This system of wide ranging contacts has left still visible traces on both the exterior and interior of buildings. This appears not only in the similarity in the conspicuous steeply-pitched straw-thatched roofs of the dwelling- and outhouses, but also in the painted panel ceilings, choir-galleries and pulpits of the Protestant churches, savouring of Renaissance influence, and in the structure of belfries and bell towers as well as in the furniture and articles used in the farmhouses.

The modest economic upward swing of the last quarter of the 19th century and the slight boom in grain production also made itself felt here. Demand for agricultural produce was growing and roads for vehicles and railroads followed the construction of systems of drains. Landscape and economy changed, though it was mostly on the larger estates that production for the market took place.

By the end of the last century the social stratification characteristic of the region had taken place: there were few paupers and comparatively many descendants of cotters and, in certain villages, the proportion of noble families was particularly high. (In the so-called noble villages, like Botpalád, Uszka or Sonkád this proportion could be as high as 60 to 80 per cent.)

The settlement structure of the village in the museum, the arrangement of the plots of ground, and the interior of the houses have been arranged with the above in mind, with the aim of presenting the way of life and social and material circumstances of the families that lived in Erdőhát in the second half of the 19th century.

The crofter's (small peasant's) *dwelling house* came to the Open Air Museum from *Kispalád* (Ill. 3). A gate of oak in the wattle fence gives access to the premises. Such gates were used for closing roads connecting villages, or leading to pastures or fields, up to the early 1900s.

Cheap and abundant local materials characterize the buildings of the homestead. The farmhouse, of room–kitchen–room arrangement, is timber-framed and its

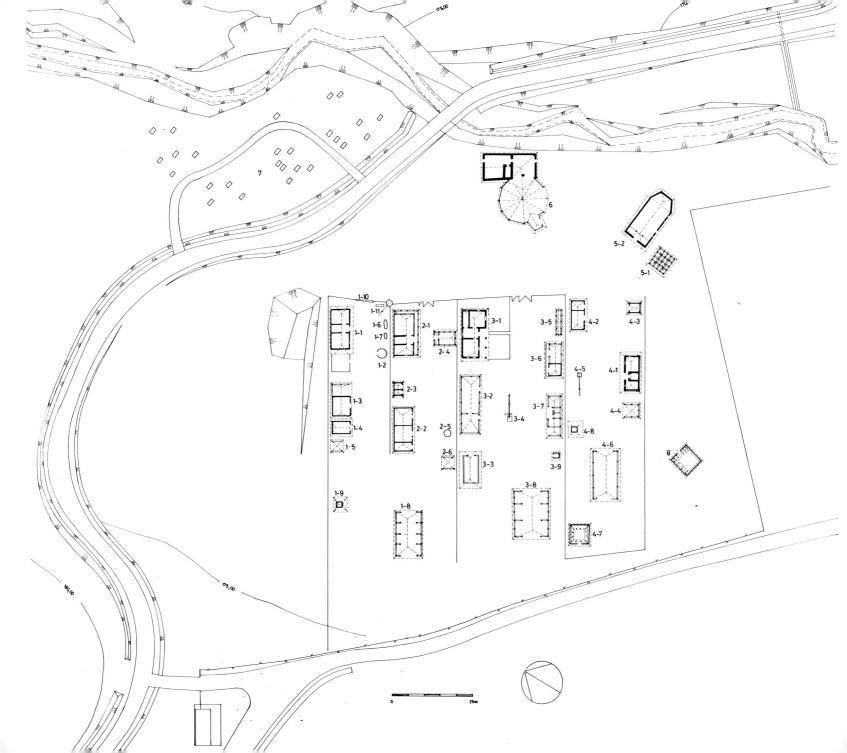

wattle walls are plastered both inside and out, with a mud and straw mixture. The timber frame surmounting the walls supported the double floor which in turn took the weight of the roof timbers. It is the sharply-sloping rafters of hewn oak, and the high, steeply-pitched, overhanging roofs of wheat-straw tightly packed against the battens attached to the rafters, that give the roofs of houses in the Upper Tisza region their peculiar character.

In the back room the beds stand, in line with the general arrangement in Erdőhát, along the walls. Under the window there is a long clothes-chest with a table in front of it. Before the beds are carved oaken chairs. Clothes could be kept in the clothes-chest and in the settle with back and arms (box settle or settle-bed standing under the window of the front room) and the dresser (almárium) held dishes. Some of the furniture, like the small backed chairs, was home-made. The beds are covered with woollen blankets, with a guba (Hungarian peasant's long, sleeveless frieze cape) serving for a pillow: this was the old folk's room. Here we can also find the most important working tools used by the women during the autumn and the winter: the loom with the warp lapped, the distaff and reel and, in a small basket, spindles, elder-tree pipes, etc.

The furniture of the front room marks the solution to housing problems that people were frequently forced to adopt when young couples starting a family lived under the same roof with the old folk and used the same kitchen. It is arranged in accordance with the traditional pattern, but includes later joiner-made pieces and textiles turned out by a factory and purchased at a fair. This is where furnishings used in bringing up children, the cradle and a baby-walker, can be found.

Each room was heated by an open hearth above which was a smoke-"bell" or funnel made of wattle plastered with mud, to lead the smoke to the smoke hole in the kitchen. The hearth was in constant use for heating, lighting, cooking and baking from late autumn until spring. Cooking in the summer took place on a bench of adobe in the kitchen, using a pot set on an iron tripod over the fire.

The wattle-walled maize shed and small henhouse, both standing on "legs" across from the house in the courtyard, were made in Kishodos, on the model of the old ones. The round, wattle-walled pigsty with its conical roof of wheat thatch has been reconstructed on the basis of the verbal description given by people from Tiszabecs.

Proceeding from the street, the stable, which is under the same roof as the vehicle shed, is the next building after the farmhouse. An ox-wagon stands in the open vehicle shed, and a beechwood chest called a hombár (granary), to hold the grain produced during the year. The wood-shed (Ill. 6) behind the stable served for storing fire-wood and was also a place for the farmer to carve his tools.

Hay was kept in the abora, a hay barn consisting of four posts and a light roof which could be raised or lowered (Ill. 4). There, after a little drying on the ground, the hay continued to be aired after being gathered. The row of outhouses is completed by the breadbaking oven.

The next farmstead, whose front building is an authentic reconstruction of a dwelling house in Botpalád, portrays the living conditions of a somewhat better-off farmer, a "middle peasant". The premises are separated from the

Master plan for the Regional Unit Representing the Upper Tisza Region
1–1: dwelling house from Kispalád; 1–2: pigsty from Tiszabecs; 1–3: stable from Kispalád; 1–4: wood shed from Botpalád; 1–5: hay-barn from Tiszabecs; 1–6: maize barn from Kishódos; 1–7: hen-house from Kishódos; 1–8: barn from Kispalád; 1–9: oven from Kispalád: 1–10: trunk-gate from Tarpa: 1–11: sweep-pole well from Tiszakóród. 2–1: dwelling house from Botpalád; 2–2: stable from Botpalád; 2–3: pigsty from Kispalád; 2–4: granary from Botpalád; 2–5: hen-house from Garbolc; 2–6: hay barn from Tiszabecs.
3–1: dwelling house from Uszka; 3–2: stable from Sonkád; 3–3: sheep pen from Botpalád; 3–4: sweep-pole well from Sonkád; 3–5: maize barn from Sonkád; 3–6: baking house from Sonkád; 3–7: pigsty from Sonkád; 3–8: barn from Sonkád; 3–9: privy from Sonkád;
4–1: dwelling house from Milota; 4–2: stable from Botpalád; 4–3: pigsty from Milota; 4–4: granary from Kispalád; 4–5: sweep-pole well from Gulács; 4–6: barn from Tiszabecs; 4–7: apiary from Botpalád; 4–8: oven from Gulács.
5–1: belfry from Nemesborzova; 5–2: Protestant church from Mánd. 6: dry mill from Vámosoroszi; 7: Protestant cemetery; 8: apiary from Panyola.

street by planking, the carved gate being an indication of the owner's importance. The house has a porch with turned wooden columns along its street front and on the side facing the courtyard. The room–kitchen–room arrangement lies within a timber-frame with wattle infill—which rests on groundsills. The partition walls are of adobe.

The first things to strike the eye of the visitor who enters the house are the glazed earthenware dishes set on the arch supporting the heavy open chimney *(szabadkémény)* of the kitchen. The large bowls were used only on the occasion of weddings or at pig-killing time. The glazed earthen-

Axonometric drawing of the dwelling house from Kispalád

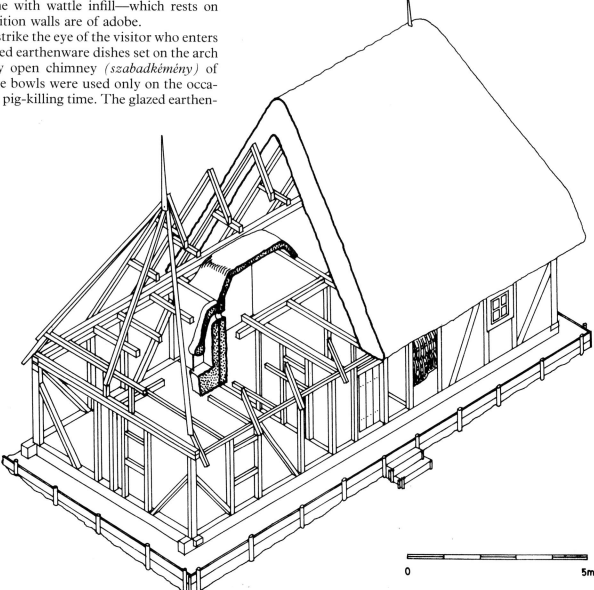

0   5m

12

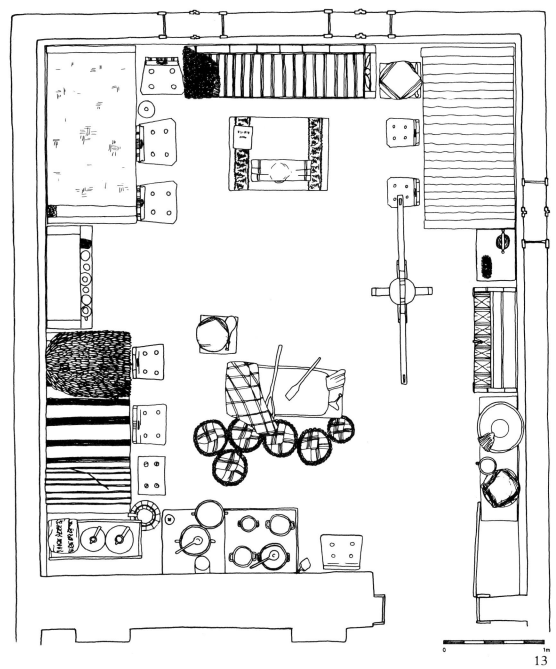

Plan for furnishing the first room
of the Botpalád house

0   1m

13

ware jugs and mugs from Nagybánya were also hung up as ornaments.

Under the vault of the open chimney stands the *bread-baking oven*. In front of it on the left is a nook where wood-ash was collected for bleaching linen. Fruit was dried in flat baskets on top of the oven, which was also used for cooking. When it had been heated up, the fireproof earthenware pot holding the food was pushed into it with a long two-pronged wrought-iron fork with two wheels, made for the purpose and called *kantaszekér* (literally "pot-cart") or *kuruglya*.

In the front from both old and new pieces of furniture can be found (Plate IV). Along the two side walls stand joiner-made beds with feather-filled covers, with a low *dikó* (narrow bed filled with straw) nearby, covered with a woollen blanket. Also made by joiners, and new at the time, are the hewn deal chest with geometric ornamentation, the painted deal dresser and the milk press *(tejesszekrény)*. Under the windows facing the street there is a wooden settle with a chest (settle-bed). Before the beds are some chairs with carved backs and tenoned legs. The most important piece of furniture is the ornately carved *almárium*, a dresser with shelves below, which was made early in the 19th century. The lower part held homespun linen and the dowry of the girl to be married, the upper part was for keeping glasses, mugs, plates and the *komaszilke* (a glazed earthenware bowl to be sent full of food to a mother in childbed). Heating and cooking took place in the room during the winter in the fireplace, which was made of adobe bricks. This was also the place where the loaves of unbaked dough were left to rise. The kneading trough, *kovászfa* ("leavening-wood"), and the baskets *szakajtó*, with the linen kerchiefs with which they were lined while holding the rising dough, were also kept here.

The back room had originally been the larder (Plate II). Around the turn of the century there were places here, the low bed from the front room and another bed, under which a small truckle-bed was kept by day. The place was used from spring to late autumn as a room in addition to its original function as pantry or larder.

Opposite the house a timber framed granary *(gabonás)* with grooved post and of board walls was erected on posts in 1889. Near the farmhouse stands the pigsty (Plate III) made of rendered oak planks with cross-headed joints. Dwelling houses, too, were built in this way in Erdőhát in the 18th century. In the long *stable*, continuing the line of house and pigsty, cattle and horses were kept in separate places. Facing the stable there is again the *abora* fox hay. At the back end of the premises of the crofter and the "middle peasant" there is an outhouse of common use, the *barn*. Its location is a sign of the continuous subdivision of holdings; it was no longer worthwhile to set up another large building on a croft half the size of the unit that used to be held in villeinage.

The *house of the gentry* transplanted from *Uszka* is separated from the street by shingled board fence. On the wicket gate, under a tiny roof by the large two-leaved gate for carts (Plate VII), the date 1906 can be read.

The whitewashed Neo-Classical front elevation, the porch with its sturdy brick pillars, and the roof of pine-wood shingles lend a dignified appearance to the home of the nobleman living off his 70–80 *holds* (37–45 hectares) of land. However, the furniture of the back room (Plate V), the kitchen which was altered at the turn of the century when the oven was transferred into the bakehouse in the courtyard, and the objects in the pantry, show equally that life carried on here did not differ fundamentally from that of the peasants.

In the *room for receiving visitors (vizit-szoba)* walnut furniture and veneered pine-wood items made by joiners can be found. The cherry-red upholstery of the "leather-covered" settee is of oilcloth. The objects in the small cupboard *(etuzsér)* have been selected with uneven taste. On the other hand, a sincere respect for tradition, the noble ancestry and the luminaries of the nation can be felt, for on the walls pictures of the family hang side by side with those of Prince Ferenc Rákóczi II, István Bocskai and a print of the laying down of arms at Világos. The papers of the family were kept in a simple little muniments' chest dating from 1837. On the shelf by the door there is a pipe, a bottle of brandy, the obligatory Bible and a prayer book. On the table the Shorter Catechism lies open.

The size of the farm is well reflected by the number and size of outbuildings. Opposite the house the first farm building as seen from the street is the timber-framed lath-walled maize shed *(kukoricagóré)*. The board-walled *granary* alongside shares the roof of the *bake-house* whose walls have been made of adobe. The timber-framed, board-walled pigsty, exceeding in size a lesser dwelling house, comprises four parts: fattening pen, droppings box, farrowing box and cart shed in that order. One of the biggest buildings on the croft, the two part *stable*, has also been made with board walls. It provided room for 15–20 horses and cattle in front of the managers. At the end of the farmyard stands the huge *threshing barn* with a *sheep-cote* (Ill. 5) roofed with thatch of trodden straw by its side.

The fourth set of premises, the so-called "cattle-yard plot" *(baromudvaros telek)* represents the most archaic part of the Upper Tisza Region. There is no fence to separate it from the street and the farmhouse is much farther inside. The front yard is occupied by the log-walled and the timber-framed *stable* with a little store room where equipment for yoking the animals was kept. The advantage of this arrangement was that the animals going out to graze and coming back in the evening did not cut up the ground in front of the house with their hooves. In the middle of the yard, near the house, stands the *granary*, the *oven* for baking bread and the *barn*.

Just like the outbuildings enumerated, the dwelling *house with adobe walls* came *from Milota*. In the room, beds stand along the side walls. Under the window there is a painted long chest made in 1830, and small chairs, with seats and backs carved from one piece of walnut wood, are placed in line in front of the beds. The smoke of the wattle-walled and plastered fireplace which heated the room was drawn through the open chimney of the kitchen. The door of the room and the pantry opens into the small ceilingless passage which is open also to the courtyard, in front of the kitchen door. The back chamber is the pantry with its timber-hewn chest for grain, another, smaller

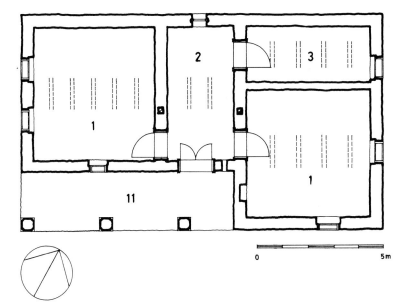

Ground plan of the Uszka dwelling house

wooden chest, flour-bags, glazed jugs for jam and other storage vessels.

Facing the dwelling house stands the *sweep-pole well from Gulács* whose carved post ends in a tulip motif. A little farther on is the courtyard *oven* under a hipped roof, similar to that of the farmhouse, supported by an open timber frame. Here, too, the farmyard is closed by a *barn* (this one has been removed to the Open Air Museum from *Tiszabecs*). Both ends of the huge structure are open: carts and waggons could go through it (Ill. 2). This was also the place where the larger farming implements were kept. Behind the farmyard, in the garden, is an *apiary* with a monopitched roof and grooved post and board walls plastered inside, containing bee-skeps made of rushes.

In the middle of the village in the Museum, in a "God's acre" hedged with lilacs, there stands a *Protestant church* with a *belfry* (Plates VIII–IX) by its side. According to the

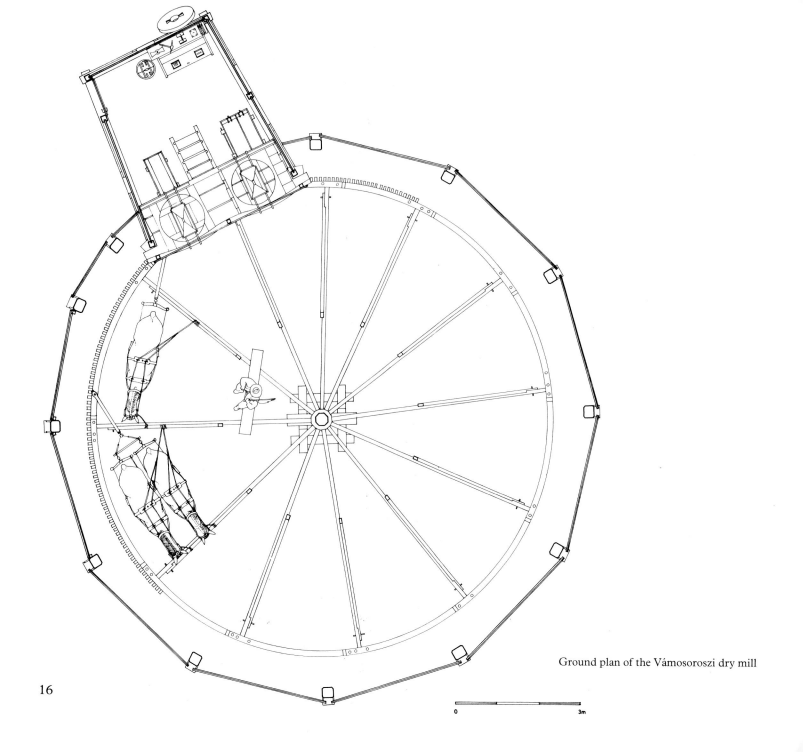

Ground plan of the Vámosoroszi dry mill

16

0   3m

inscription on one of the ceiling panels, the church was built in 1790 in the place of an earlier one, in Mánd. It, too, is timber-framed and wattle-walled like the majority of the farmhouses and outbuildings. The interior of the church is divided into two by an archivolt. Its painted, coffered ceiling, and the remarkably beautiful crown-shaped canopy, sawn, carved and painted, represent a late version of the painted interiors of 18th–19th century Protestant churches.

The belfry, standing detached from the church, is supposed to have been built of oak in *Nemesborzova* in the 18th century (Ill. 7). The date of the tin flag that acts as a weather-cock on one of its small turrets is 1794.

It was after the enactment of the Edict of Tolerance late in the 18th century that the parishes of the Calvinist Church began to be better off. By the middle of the 19th century more and more of them obtained a liquor licence, and built or acquired a "dry mill" (a kind of horse-walk used for purposes other than threshing). This is why the "dry mill" of the Vécsey estate at Csegöld was transferred to *Vámosoroszi* in 1846 (Plate X). When it failed to earn the expected income, an oil press was added to it forty years later. The mill, taken down and re-erected in the museum, consists of three parts: the "milling house" where grinding and the scouring of millet seed took place, the oil mill, where the oilseed was decorticated, crushed, roasted and pressed, and between them, the "engine-shed" or horse-walk, where the huge wooden wheel was turned horizontally by two or three horses. This wheel was fitted with 370 wooden cogs to set the pairs of grinding and scouring stones in motion, and also the upper stone of the decorticator *(hajaló)*.

Not far from the buildings described above, the wooden *graveposts* taken from the old Protestant cemetery in *Szatmárcseke* can be seen, made by a traditional method that is still practised. The pentagonal stems, carved from huge oaks, taper off and end in a pointed edge. The outer side of the grave posts, set up by eastward-orientated tombs, was painted black and inscribed with a rhyming epitaph giving a short summary of the deceased's life. The characters were engraved on the wooden surface with a special pen for inscribing graveposts *(fejfaíró penna)*.

The purpose of this part of the Open Air Museum is not only to demonstrate the vernacular culture of a territory that is definable in geographical terms, but also the *szálláskertes* settlement structure. Its main characteristic is that the dwelling houses stand in the centre of the village without any visible order of arrangement (Ill. 8), without associated farmyards behind the houses; the outbuildings can be found in the "gardens" *(kertek)*, which often form a ring around the nucleus of living quarters. This form of settlement, whose origins were under discussion until recently, is known not only in the geographical Central Tisza region, but over a much larger area, practically all over the Great Hungarian Plain. Besides this, we want to give a picture of the territory where the type of dwelling house usual in Northern Hungary met the one typical of the Great Plain, and to show the intricate historical process in the course of which the latter gained ground. To satisfy these aims, the southern part of Borsod County proved to be the most fruitful area of collecting. Recent research has revealed that the form of settlement characterized by such outsteadings took shape in this area early in the 18th century (practically after the Turkish forces of occupation had been expelled), and was called to life primarily by a specific type of farming. Its disintegration began in the earlier half of the 19th century and its total disappearance in the 1870s.

Here and there even 18th century structures could be found in the southern part of Borsod County, like the *Nemesbikk parish hall* and the *house from Igrici.*

The settlement in the museum represents a village with outsteadings. The parish hall stands in the middle around it, surrounded by the board-fenced, irregular yards characteristic of agglomerated settlements *(halmazos települések)*. In the ring of outsteadings surrounding the agglomerated nucleus, the plots are larger, and the fences are different. Adobe fences face the street, and at the end of the gardens dense hedgerows of boxthorn (Lycium sp.) indicate the border.

The majority of buildings have already been dismantled and are stored within the confines of the Museum, awaiting re-erection.

The centre of the Museum village will be the *parish hall* removed from *Nemesbikk* (Ill. 9). In all probability it stood as long ago as the end of the 18th century, but it is documented from the second half of the 19th century. The building, erected of large adobe bricks, differs in no way from the mansion houses of the less well-to-do gentry which were erected in the same period. Proceeding from the porch we enter an area stretching up to the other end of the house; over the central part of this an open chimney used to stand, supported by two arches. From the back of this inside area the visitor can enter a stonevaulted cellar by raising a stone slab; this, according to the villagers' recollections, used to be a jail. Behind the main front, there is, on each side, a big room with a narrower one behind. The one on the left of the entrance was the board room. Its roof had been covered, up to the 1920s, with shingles. The doors and windows of the parish hall date from the second half of the 19th century.

The oldest building dismantled that can be dated is the *dwelling house from Igrici* (Ill. 11). It was erected in 1776 of large adobe bricks, the lowest row of which was laid immediately on the levelled ground. At the time it was taken down, the ground plan of the house was the same as at the end of the 18th century: the kitchen door opened on the yard and from the kitchen the room could be entered in one direction and the pantry in the other. The central beam under the ceiling-cum-loft floor had been length-

Master plan for the regional unit representing the Central Tisza Region.
1: dwelling house from Igrici; 2–1: dwelling house from Mezőkövesd; 2–2: pigsty from Mezőkövesd.
3: dwelling house from Tiszatarján; 4–1: dwelling house from Mezőcsát; 4–2: summer kitchen from Oszlár; 4–3: pigsty from Mezőcsát; 5: dwelling house from Mezőkövesd.
6: parish hall from Nemesbikk; 7: stable with fireplace from Tiszatarján; 8: stable with fireplace from Mezőkövesd; 9: stable with fireplace from Mezőcsát; 10: stable with fireplace from Mezőkövesd.

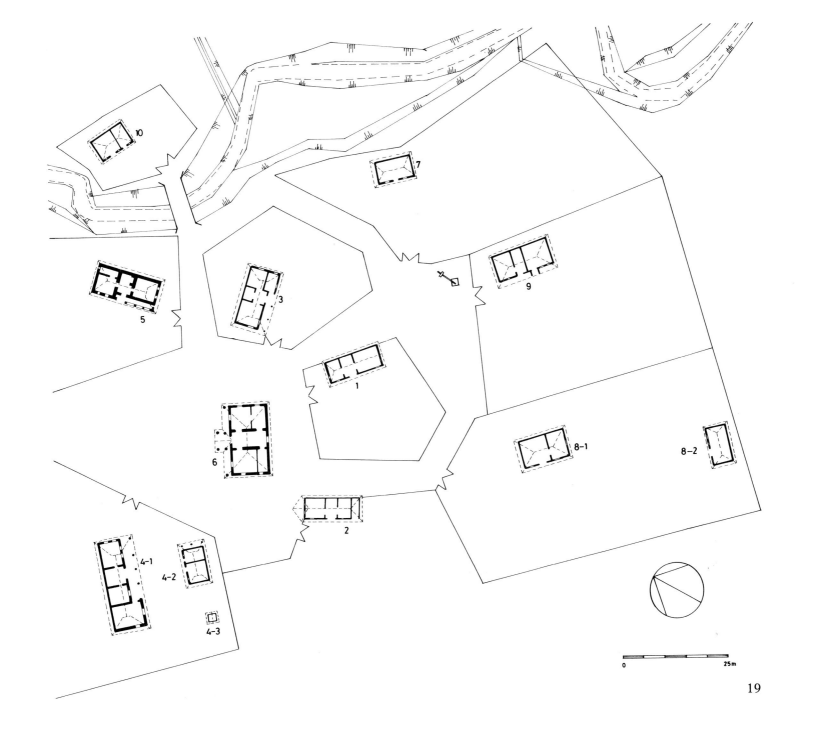

19

ened and neither the ceiling boarding not its mud cover was uniform over the two parts of the building. On the basis of this and other knowledge gained during the dismantling, it can be supposed that at the time it was built there was no loft over the pantry, as in several examples in the neighbouring villages. The rafters rested against the ridge pole, which was supported by three Y-shaped oak uprights, the first of which stood by the end of the room, the second by the wall between the room and the kitchen, and the third by the wall separating the kitchen and pantry. The ridge pole was of pine. The traces of timber spikes on it show that it must have been transported on the river Tisza as part of a raft to one of the raft ports near Igric. The hipped end over the short pantry extension is also worthy of note.

When the house was taken down, the fireplaces were no longer in their original state. As the former owner informed us, a fire-bench used to stand in the middle *(középpadka)*, under the open chimney, which had by then been replaced by a loft. We were pleasantly surprised to find in the trial trench a well-burned layer of clay with a distinct outline not far from the surface. On this basis we could reconstruct the former "heating installation" of the kitchen: the rectangular oven under the chimney with a cauldron-stand *(katlan, üstház)* on top. In the room the large stack-shaped earthenware oven *(boglyakemence)*, built on top of a solid clay ledge of the usual height and made of daubed wickerwork, was still in its place.

Accordingly, when the house was built, or in an early stage of its history, there were two closed ovens in it, which reminds us of the 16th century houses excavated in the neighbourhood of Kecskemét. Therefore we may rightly consider the house from Igric as one of the remaining structures modelled on the type prevailing in the Great Hungarian Plain in the late Middle Ages.

The characteristic shape of the roof of the so-called *üstökös ház* ("forelock" house) from *Mezőkövesd* (Ill. 10) will be reconstructed when the building is put up again in the museum grounds. It used to stand in the central residential nucleus, still visibly an agglomeration of houses of

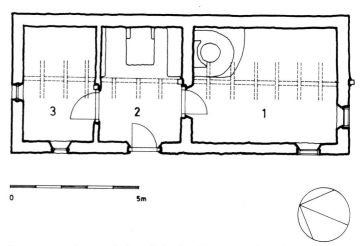

Reconstructed ground plan of the dwelling house from Igrici

Mezőkövesd and, although we do not know its exact date, it must have been built in the first third of the 19th century.

Originally the house consisted of a room, a kitchen, a pantry and a shed. At the time of dismantling the last did not stand any more; its place was indicated by the remains of a wall. This house, too, was built of adobe bricks, and the level of its floor was below that of the courtyard. The ceiling was made of reeds spread over joists, plastered thinly below and thickly covered with mud above.

Here, too, part of the weight of the roof timber was carried by Y-shaped uprights and the ridge pole supported by them. A little above the level of the windows, a mortise in the upright nearest the street and a cut at the end of the ridge pole, gave evidence of the earlier form of roofing. A rafter was fastened by a wooden peg to the notch at the end of the ridge pole; this rafter by a raker fitted into the mortise found in the upright and their meeting point was also supported from two directions by more slender rafters, whose other ends rested on the wall plates that ran along the top of the wall and projected over the face of the house. With this we have the picture of the characteristic protruding "forelock" roofing, covered by reeds. The place under it was once a favourite haunt of both old and young.

The front room with the oven in the Mezőkövesd house was the place where the family lived. The pantry, however, was not only used for storage but also as the bedroom of the young woman. This custom, along with some structural features, shows that the forms of dwelling houses and the ways of using them in the Great Hungarian Plain and in the northern hilly country prevailed with equal force in Mezőkövesd.

The dwelling houses that made up the nucleus of Mezőkövesd were mostly occupied by *summások* (agricultural labourers who toured the country in gangs offering their services on a contract basis for seasonal jobs), who lived in the last years of the 19th century. This period is represented by the entire Central Tisza region in the Open Air Museum. By that time the farmers had moved, as a result of the disintegration of the characteristic house and outsteading *(szálláskertes)* form of settlement. The outsteadings became the new nuclei, and people built their new houses there. The house taken down in Honvéd Street might well have belonged to a farmer when built, but in the period represented by its reconstruction in the Museum, it was already inhabited by a family of seasonal contract labourers.

The way of life of "middle peasants" will be presented by the *Tiszatarján house* (Ill. 12) erected around 1850–60. Here, too, the walls were made of adobe and the floor plan shows a room and kitchen and a porch with wooden posts. The porch only stretches as far as the end of the kitchen and the next part is divided, parallel with the longitudinal axis of the house, into room and pantry. The former is entered from the area in front of the kitchen, the latter from the end of the porch.

Nothing has remained of the original heating devices of the building. When taking down the angular oven in the room we found its stack-shaped predecessor *(boglyakemence)*. Till around 1920 the small back room was also heated with such an oven. On the two sides of the kitchen there was a ledge in front of the mouth of each oven and in the middle there was a somewhat higher fire-ledge *(középpadka)* which here, too, was called *konyha* (kitchen). The open chimney of daubed wickerwork was standing in place even at the time when the house was taken down.

Two discoveries were made then: the earlier window of the house, placed symmetrically with the one looking onto the street, and the old, timber-framed doorway *(ácstokos ajtó)*, bridged by a little arch, in the front room. It had been hidden by the lining of the door frame, and matched the door of the back room.

This type of building is fairly usual in Tiszatarján; in the street formed in the place of one-time outsteadings, there are several of them. In the earlier agglomerated central dwelling quarter, however, we look for such structures in vain.

The *houses of petty nobles* to be represented in the museum by a building from *Mezőcsát* (Ill. 15) had also become general in the 1850s. The one chosen for transplantation has adobe walls but the porch was made, as its owner has told us, of bricks. A roof of rafters and collar beams was made of pine. The hipped roof, with a small smoke hole at each end, is covered with reed fastened to the roof battens with withes. The stack-shaped oven in the back room is the original one but the front room was heated with an iron stove. In the kitchen, a built-in cooking range *(berakott masina)* used to stand by the long wall at the back.

Buildings with the same ground plan of room, kitchen, room, with a porch in front and a granary spanning the whole width of the house, can be found in Mezőcsát and also in other settlements in the southern part of Borsod County. In Mezőkövesd, however, the Mezőcsát archetype was reshaped in a characteristic way. The roof is not hipped at the street front, but there is a straight plank gable wall abundantly ornamented with applied motifs in timber. The window frames are often made of ashlar topped by a semicircle of ornamentation in plaster. The cylindrical posts of the porch have been replaced by squared pillars with just a plank railing, instead of a wall, between them (Plate XII). The arches, too, have become lighter (Ill. 17); they do not carry weight any more and their only role is that of ornamentation.

All this fits well into the formation of vernacular styles in the 19th century, of which another good architectural representation will be the *house* of the substantial farmer from *Mezőkövesd*. This building, together with its furniture, will show well the similarities and differences between the ways of life of the lowest and uppermost layers of peasantry, that is to say agricultural labourers and rich farmers in the same place and period.

Up to now we have dealt with houses standing in the central dwelling quarter of the ensemble representing the Central Tisza region, where farm buildings can hardly be found. At the time represented in the Museum reconstructions, however, disintegration of the earlier form of settlement had already started and certain outbuildings had begun to appear in the courtyards of dwelling houses. Of these we plan to transplant *two pigsties*, and four versions of the *stable with fireplace (tüzelősól)* (Ill. 16–17), which were the most important buildings of the outsteading. The most archaic of them from *Mezőcsát* has a huge protruding entrance, with two windbreak walls by the door. The stables of more or less similar construction (adobe walls with rafter roof covered with reeds) were not only for housing animals but, in Mezőkövesd, were also the place for men to sleep. They only went to the house in the centre of the village for the main meals of the day. The characteristic built-in furniture of the stable was the *tüzelő* ("firing") comprising plank beds standing around the fireplace which was made of and surrounded by stones or adobe bricks.

In the outsteading where the stable of the rich Mezőkövesd farmer will be re-erected, a chaff barn *(pelyvatartó)* (Ill. 14) of adobe walls and a ridge pole roof covered with reed and supported by Y-shaped uprights will also be put up. This was the place to store the *garmada,* grain trodden out but not yet winnowed, in olden times when grain was obtained by treading or trampling out.

22

The largest section of the Open Air Museum covers two important regions of the Great Hungarian Plain, the one between the rivers Danube and Tisza, and the southern part of the territory east of the Tisza. The most characteristic features of these large regions are the market towns that took shape in the 18th–19th centuries.

Urban development was determined in East-Central Europe at that time by specialization in producing agricultural products (meat and live-stock, wool, wine and grain) for the market, and its general characteristic was absolute and comparative overpopulation (never in the course of Hungarian history did agro-towns outstrip industrial ones as much as in this particular period). It was these factors that brought about the extensive forms of settlements (auxiliary settlements, *tartozéktelepülések,* consisting of outsteadings, vineyards and, especially, detached farmsteads). It was also characteristic of these market towns that they fulfilled administrative, commercial, industrial (especially in the field of food processing), educational and social functions. The museum's task, therefore, was to find ways of demonstrating the territorial, social and economic connections characterized by a certain type of agricultural development over two centuries. It was in this period that the geographical features and landscape of the Great Hungarian Plain assumed their present appearance in the wake of anti-inundation works, draining and the regulation of riverways. At the same time the composition of its population (Hungarian plus German, Serb, Slovak and Romanian minorities) took form and the division of the inhabitants according to their financial status and place in the division of labour evolved.

Present plans for the museum "region" envisage presenting the picture of a market town in the Great Hungarian Plain in the 18th–19th centuries through 53 characteristic buildings on 33 crofts. This will include the following forms of settlement structure:

(1) Agglomerated unit representing both the earlier houses untouched by settlement development and the crowdedness resulting from the breaking up of plots in the centre of the town. Houses showing the living conditions of agricultural labourers, poor peasants, smallholders and "middle peasants" will be on view here, together with a scientifically reconstructed dwelling of reed walls from Sárrét.

(2) A street consisting of rows of houses showing the situation after the re-settlement in the 18th century and development plans in the 19th. These buildings will at the same time acquaint visitors with the way of life of better-off farmers and petty nobles as well as with the workshops and tools of some craftsmen: a manor house from Karcag (Ill. 19), a house inhabited by Slovak farmers from Mezőberény, a petty noble's home from Hajdúbagos, a manor house from Tótkomlós (Ill. 21) and a potter's house from Hódmezővásárhely.

(3) Another important part of the plan is the foursided square which had become characteristic of market towns.

(4) The buildings of the fringes of the market town—the inn, tanner's house and, separated a little, the Protestant cemetery—are organically connected to the inner quarters in respect of both place and function.

(5) The vast peripheral areas will be presented by buildings which were in actuality far more distant from the town: vineyard huts, horticultural detached farmsteads from the vicinity of Szeged, grain producing ones from Békés county, windmills from Dusnok and Kunhegyes and, finally, the floating Ráckeve boat-mill *(hajómalom),* a piece of great interest for the history of engineering.

Of the buildings chosen for the Market Town in the Great Hungarian Plain twenty have already been dismantled. Re-erection began with the tanner's house from Baja in 1986.

Replicas and reconstructions also figure in the settlement plan. In relocating certain objects consideration must be made for the fact that only a part of the materials obtained in dismantling will be useable for the actual relocation. Designs and other documentation preserved at

Master plan for the regional unit representing market towns in the Great Hungarian Plain

1–1: dwelling house from Berekböszörmény; 1–2: stable from Méhkerék; 1–3: granary from Méhkerék; 2–1: dwelling house from Hajdúbagos; 2–2: stable from Szeghalom; 3–1: dwelling house from Tótkomlós; 3–2: granary from Tótkomlós; 4–1: dwelling house from Békés; 4–2: granary from Orosháza; 5: dwelling house from Makó; 6–1: dwelling house from Karcag; 6–2: stable from Karcag; 7: dwelling house from Hódmezővásárhely; 8: dwelling house from Baja; 9: dwelling house from Szentes; 10: dwelling house from Debrecen; 11: dwelling house from Debrecen; 12: dwelling house from Hajdúnánás; 13: reed house from the Great Hungarian Plain (reconstruction); 14: dwelling house from Nagykőrös; 15: dwelling house from Jászárokszállás; 16: dwelling house from Szegvár; 17–1: dwelling house from Dömsöd; 17–2: pigsty from Dömsöd; 17–3: well from Dömsöd; 18–1: dwelling house from Dunapataj; 18–2: pigsty from Dunapataj; 18–3: well from Dunapataj; 19: tavern from Kiskunhalas; 20–1: dwelling house from Uszód; 20–2: stable from Uszód; 21–1: dwelling house from Mezőberény; 21–2: granary from Békéscsaba; 22: dwelling house from Cegléd; 23–1: dwelling house from Fülöpszállás; 23–2: storage chamber for wine from Fülöpszállás; 23–3: farm labourers' dwelling house and stable from Fülöpszállás; 24: dwelling house from Homokmégy; 25–1: inn from Jászárokszállás; 25–2: stable from Jászárokszállás; 25–3: cartshed from Jászárokszállás; 26: tannery from Baja; 27–1: dwelling house from Konyár; 27–2: planked pigsty from Konyár; 28–1: windmill from Kunhegyes; 28–2: miller's house from Kunhegyes; 29: windmill from Dusnok; 30: detached farmstead unit from Csongrád; 31: shed from a Hajdúság vineyard; 32: hut from a Solt vineyard; 33: protestant cemetery; 34: caretaker's house in the cemetery

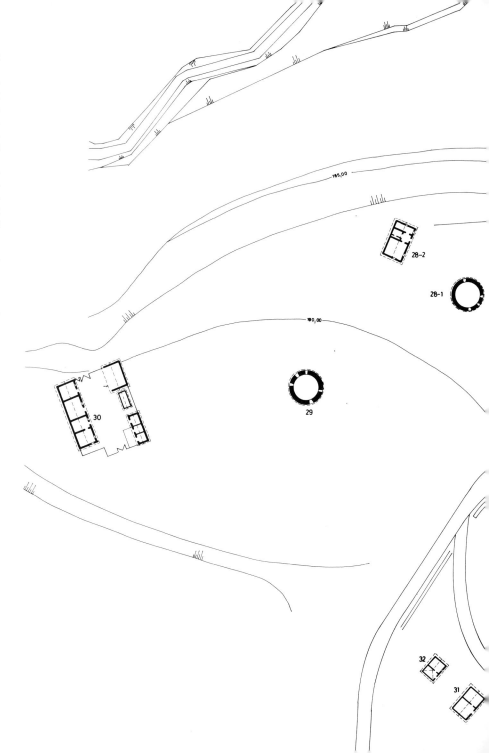

council technical repositories may also be useful in some cases. Dating from 1883, there is the design of a Debrecen burgher house reconstructed as a part of a town planning project (Plate XIII, Ill. 20).

(1) The *dwelling house* in the agglomerated part from *Dunapataj* is to show how a family of agricultural labourers built and furnished their home in the second half of the 19th century. The curtilage was on the fringe of the settlement, by the dam in the flood plain of the Danube. The house, comprising a room, kitchen and pantry, stood in a corner of its courtyard with the pantry facing the street. The last was also used as a room to live in from time to time and was then heated from the kitchen. The walls were of wattle and daub, the partition walls of adobe. The central beam along the longitudinal axis of the house was supported by short Y-shaped uprights. The wooden frame prepared in this way was then plastered with mud mixed with straw, and smoothed. The material of the ceiling was pine, and the ceiling over the pantry was covered with reeds. On the rear side of the open chimney is the date 1889. It may be presumed that the house originally had a chimneyless kitchen (*füstös konyha* = "smoky" kitchen) with a smoke "bell" (*szikrafogó*, device to keep sparks off the roof). The rafters rested on a ridge-pole supported by Y-shaped pine uprights and were covered with reeds. The truncated cone-shaped oven in the room was heated from the fire ledge in the kitchen. On the left of the ledge there was a simple brick-walled cauldron-stand.

The *house from Homokmégy* was originally built in 1875 on the outsteading of a well-to-do farmer ("middle peasant") whose main occupation was to keep animals. The original arrangement of the building was room, kitchen, room, pantry, stable and another stable with a porch of wooden posts along the front facing the farmyard. A horizontal layer of reeds was applied at every 40–50 cm to reinforce the rammed earth walling. The planked ceiling over the central beam *(mestergerendás pórfödém)* was topped with a layer of reeds which was then covered with mud about 10–15 cm thick. The collared roof was also covered with reeds. The street front of the house was ornamented with a sun-ray motif made of sawn pine boards.

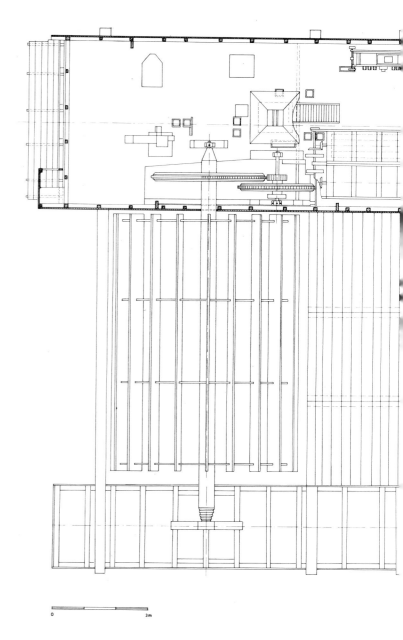

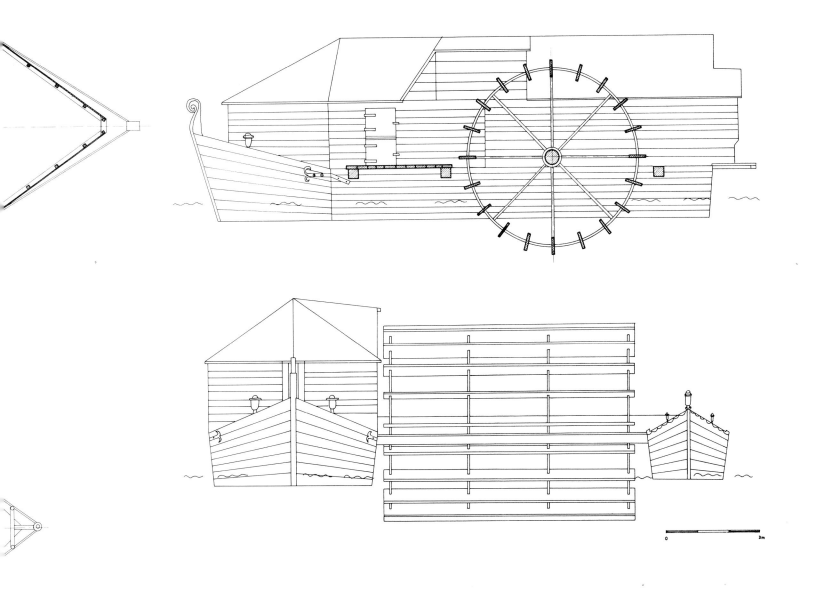

Ground plan, side and front-views of the boat mill from Ráckeve

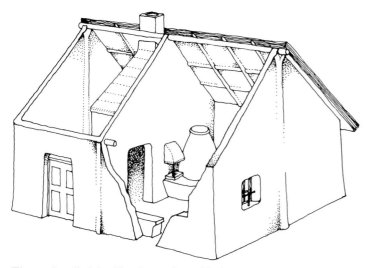

The reed-walled dwelling house from Sárrét (reconstruction drawing)

The *house* removed from *Konyár,* was one of the oldest dwellings in the village and stood in the agglomerated nucleus. The state of the building at the time when it was taken down suggested several phases of reconstruction since it was erected late in the 18th century. It had white-washed adobe walls, a board gable and a porch with wooden posts along the side facing the courtyard. The floor was of beaten earth, and the roof was thatched. In the kitchen there was a ledge for the fire under the open chimney and the room was heated by an oven. The arrangement of the building was room, kitchen (whose fire-place was under an open chimney, *kéményalja*, where it opened onto a small passage, *pitvar*, open to the roof and entered from the courtyard), and pantry. Its furniture will show that it used to be inhabited by families of the poorest social strata, servants and agricultural labourers.

The *house from Jászárokszállás* is, with its adobe walls, saddle roof covered with reeds, room–kitchen–pantry arrangement and two-windowed plastered street-front gable, a typical example of a Central Hungarian dwelling in the Great Hungarian Plain. The furnished building will present the household of a peasant working as a bootmaker in the winter at the end of the 19th century.

The archaic building methods of some areas in the Great Hungarian Plain will be demonstrated by the *Dömsöd house*. Its cab-walls are topped with a reed-covered saddle roof resting on a ridge-pole supported by Y-shaped uprights. The ground plan arrangement of the L-shaped building is room, kitchen, pantry, and a storage chamber for wine. It will represent the way of life on the farm of a "middle peasant" who also owned a vineyard by the river Danube at the end of the 19th century.

The *house from Szegvár* is one of the basic forms of peasant house in the southern part of the territory east of the river Tisza (Ill. 18). The arrangement of the building is room, kitchen, pantry, stable. The walls are made of adobe blocks and the saddle roof, covered by reed, rests on a ridge pole supported by scissors beams or *ollóágas*. The kitchen is equipped with a fire bench and cauldron-stand below the open chimney and in the room there is a large stack-shaped earthenware oven, or *búbos kemence*.

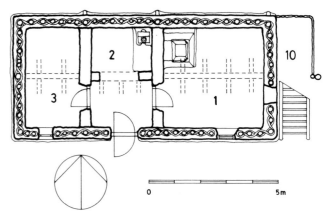

Ground plan of the Dunapataj dwelling house (revealed when taking down the building)

28

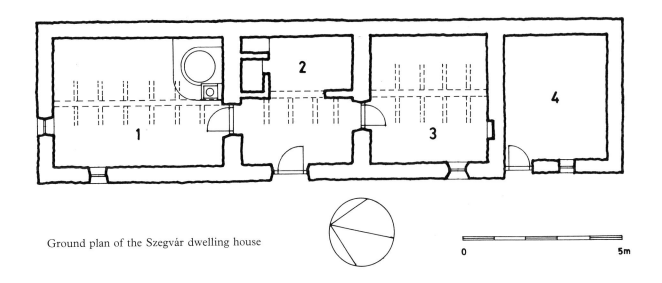

Ground plan of the Szegvár dwelling house

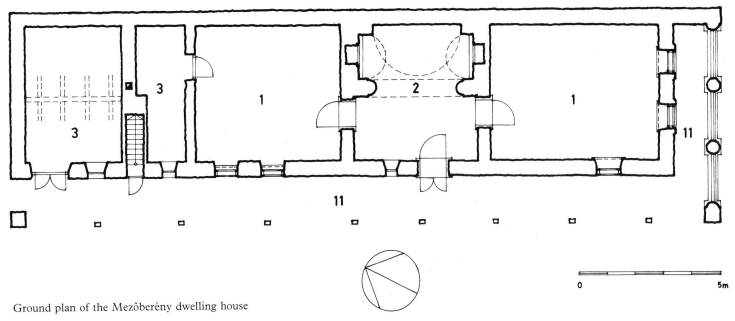

Ground plan of the Mezőberény dwelling house

29

There is one window on the street front and a wooden fence abuts the walls of the building. The unadorned, brown, peasant furniture, which is locally made and arranged in the corners, reflects the social-economic level of poor peasants in the 1880s. In the pantry there are the paraphernalia of basket making, a home craft pursued to supplement the earnings of the family.

(2) In the unit of settlement arranged in the form of a street the *house from Mezőberény* is typical of the villages inhabited by Slovaks in the Great Hungarian Plain. On the street front there is a porch with wrought-iron grids between its plastered cylindrical columns. The gable-end, made of brick, is ornamented with plaster. The walls are of adobe blocks, and the saddle roof is covered with tiles. In the kitchen there is an open chimney above the fire ledge, and each room is heated with an oven. Along the wall facing the courtyard a veranda can be seen. A peculiarity of the ground plan of the house is the pantry opening from the second room. The building clearly shows from its size alone, that it was owned by a well-to-do farmer. This is confirmed by the fact that a detached farmstead in the fields of the village belonged to it. At the end of the house the *cart shed* and the *stable* stand under the same ridge. The importance of growing grain crops is demonstrated by the brick *granary* with tiled saddle roof and cellar. The furniture of the house will demonstrate the culture and living conditions of rich Slovak peasants in the Great Hungarian Plain.

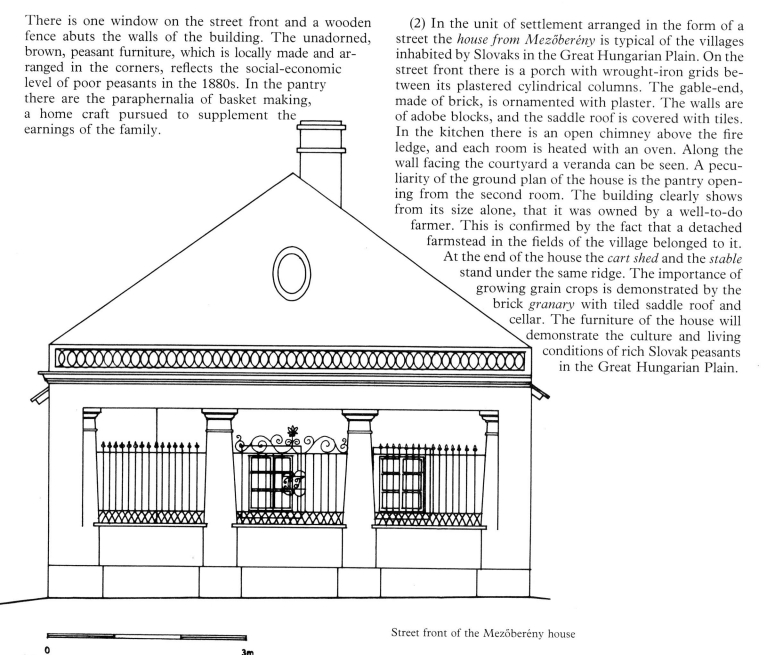

Street front of the Mezőberény house

0   3m

30

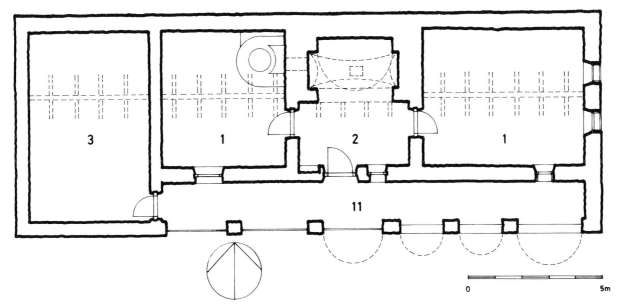

Ground plan of the Hajdúbagos dwelling house

The building of *Hajdúbagos* is a good example of Neo-Classic *houses* in the Hajdúság inhabited by families of gentry origin but living a peasant's life. It stands at the end of the village with its façade facing the main street and its courtyard and garden turned to the path leading towards the fields. There are two windows in the whitewashed wall of the street front and two ventilation holes surrounded by plaster moulding *(vakolatkeretes)* in the attic. The side facing the courtyard is accompanied by the six posts of the veranda whose open end is visible from the street. The walls are built of adobe blocks, the so-called small-hipped saddle roof is covered with reed. The floor is of beaten earth but the ceilings with their planed beam and cladding meet more exacting demands. The arrangement of the building is room, kitchen (with its fireplace under the open chimney, opening onto a small passage, *pitvar*, reaching to the roof and open for its full width to the Yard), another room, and pantry. The pantry, which is as long as the house is wide, opens off the veranda and holds a big

built-in, two-part fir wood container for grain *(hambár)*. The courtyard with its *stable, barn, pigsty* and *maize shed* reflects a farm where animal husbandry and plant production are well balanced.

Hódmezővásárhely, the market town lying in the Great Hungarian Plain and famous for its potters, will be represented by a house which for long also accommodated a *pottery*. It gained its final form in 1904, as an L-shaped corner house. The main building, facing the street, was already standing in 1880. It was those days that the street "under the dam" was built, where many potters lived and worked. The main building with its wide porch gives on to the street with and asymmetrically placed window and a sawn-plank gable. Its walls are made of adobe bricks and its gabled, collared roof is covered by tiles. Before the annexe was erected at right angles to the old building, the kiln had been in the kitchen.

The *buildings* standing in an unbroken row *on a croft (zárt beépítésű telek) in Fülöpszállás* are still in their orig-

31

inal place in the quarter named Büge where in days gone by the outsteadings stood in their gardens. The farmhouse and the outbuilding standing parallel to it were erected, according to the inscription on the main beam, in 1830. The storage chamber for wine between the two, was constructed later. On one of the long sides of the farmhouse, whose arrangement is room, kitchen, room and pantry, there is an arcaded veranda with a sawn-plank parapet on a matching scale. The roof timbers of the building, which has a gable of planks, rest on a ridge pole supported by scissors beams and is covered by reed. In the outbuilding facing the house a *stable*, a *farm labourer's dwelling* and a *cart shed* can be found. The group from Fülöpszállás aims at presenting the way of life of the rich farmer who keeps farm hands all the year round.

(3) The house from Baja, which will be re-erected to look as it did in the second half of the 19th century, will stand in one corner of the market town square. The selected *dwelling house*, whose façade was ornamented with plaster, became the property of a Serb corn merchant between 1850 and 1860. Most probably the corn loft dates back to this time. The shorter wing of the building, of L-shaped ground plan, is divided in two by a gateway. On its right there are living quarters (originally the servants' quarters) consisting of room and kitchen, and on the left there are four rooms, a kitchen and a pantry, connected by the arcaded veranda that separates the house from the courtyard. The roof with its two queen-posts *(kétállószékes)* over the brick-and-adobe compound walls, is the work of a trained carpenter and is covered by plain tiles.

The furniture will represent the highest level of the market town burgher's taste in interior decoration at the time of the grain boom.

In the hindmost room on the courtyard side of the *house from Szentes* there used to be a hat-maker's workshop. The shop and the store for finished goods occupied smaller rooms opening on the street. The foundations and the cellar of the L-shaped building, as well as the pillars and arches of its porch, were made of burnt bricks whereas the walls above ground were of adobe. The street front has an

elaborate ornamentation in plaster, and the rest of the wall surfaces are simply whitewashed. The queen-post roof *(állószékes)* has been renewed, and the saddle roof is covered with tiles. The street front is connected to the neighbouring building by an arched gate, and the courtyard side is in proportion to the pillars and arches of the porch. The ceilings are either timbered or plastered *(sík-mennyezetű)* and the floors range from earth through stone flag to planked floor. The arrangement of the reconstructed ground plan, starting from the street gate, will be as follows: store for finished goods, business premises, "clean room" *(tisztaszoba)*, kitchen, living room and workshop.

Since 1868 the building had been owned by the Csuray dynasty of hat-makers who gave, in the course of about a century, seven master hatters to the town. They also had about 10 holds (5.7 hectares) of land with a small detached farmstead, where they farmed on a modest scale.

The *house from Makó* was erected between 1860 and

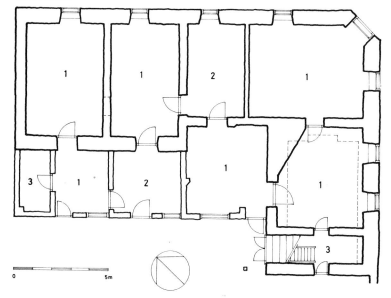

Ground plan of the Kiskunhalas tavern when it was built and when it was taken down

1880 in more than one stage. It represents a type of architecture, widely accepted in the market towns of the Great Hungarian Plain, which enables the portrayal of the change in the way of life of the peasant-burgher stratum through the interior decoration applied by them and leading to the formation of a local style. The group of buildings will also demonstrate a characteristic form of agricultural enterprise based on the monoculture of onions.

The arrangement of the groundplan is: small room, street room, anteroom (kitchen), inner room, back kitchen and pantry. The small room and the pantry are connected in the same level by a pillared porch, as was usual in the area. The house has mud walls with the pillars and parapet of the porch made of locally burnt bricks. The walls were plastered both outside and in, then whitewashed and painted respectively. There are three windows on the street front which is broken up, more or less symmetrically, by four pilasters *(lizénás oszlop)*. The stucco strings and frames on the façade are important stylistic elements of the Neo-Classic vernacular architecture of the time. The up-

per edge of the gable is decorated with locally made glazed ceramic balls. The pillars of the whitewashed wall separating the premises from the street and appearing as an organic continuation of the street front of the house, are also decorated by ceramic balls. The saddle roof with queen-

Cross-section of the Baja tanner's house

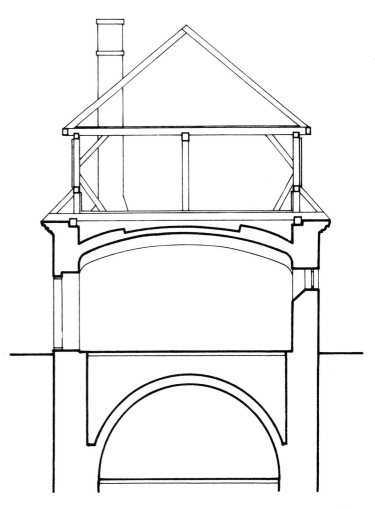

33

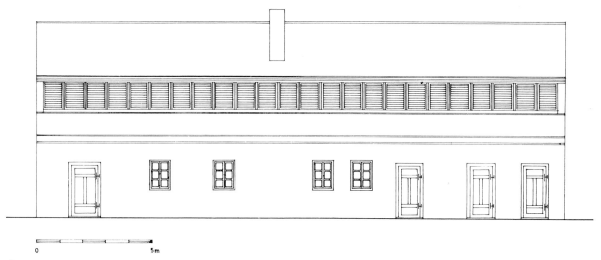

Courtyard front and cross-section of the tanner's house in Baja

posts rests on two wall plates and is covered with plain tiles. The loft floors are different from place to place. In each room there is a stack-shaped oven, with internally accessible flue *(kaminos kémény)* characteristic of the Great Hungarian Plain, and in the back kitchen there is a cooking range made of bricks, with wrought iron doors and fittings.

The *dwelling house with tavern from Kiskunhalas* was built on the corner of a street junction in the middle of the 19th century. The tavern operated up to the late 1880s, when it was converted into a dwelling. The L-shaped building originally consisted of the tavern (taproom, private room, pantry) and a dwelling unit consisting of room and kitchen, with a porch on the yard street front of the former. The room was heated by a stack-shaped oven through the internally accessible flue *(kaminkémény)* of the kitchen, on the ledge of which cooking took place. The tap room, private room, pantry and cellar were connected by the porch, onto which also opened the corner hatch window of the kitchen, through which meals were handed out, and from which the tavern was heated. The big chim-

ney occupying a corner of the private room constituted an interesting transition between the open chimney and the closed internally accessible flue *(kamin)*. It was completely open at the bottom; standing under the chimney one could heat the big stack-shaped ovens in the room and the taproom. When the building was taken down, it came to light that the thick outer mud walls of the house had been erected first, followed by the cross walls of the same material alternating with adobe in the more tricky places. An interesting feature of the ceiling was that the space between the beams was filled with wooden rods wrapped in straw *(szalmapólyás födém)* and there was a complicated distribution of beams *(gerendakiosztás)* on the corner near the porch. The collared roof was made of sawn deal. On the battens under the tiles marks of an earlier wooden shingling were found.

(4) The *tannery from Baja*, which has been chosen to represent a branch of the handicraft trades that was of major importance in the region between the rivers Danube and Tisza up to the end of the 19th century, will be located on the southern side of the museum unit that gives visitors

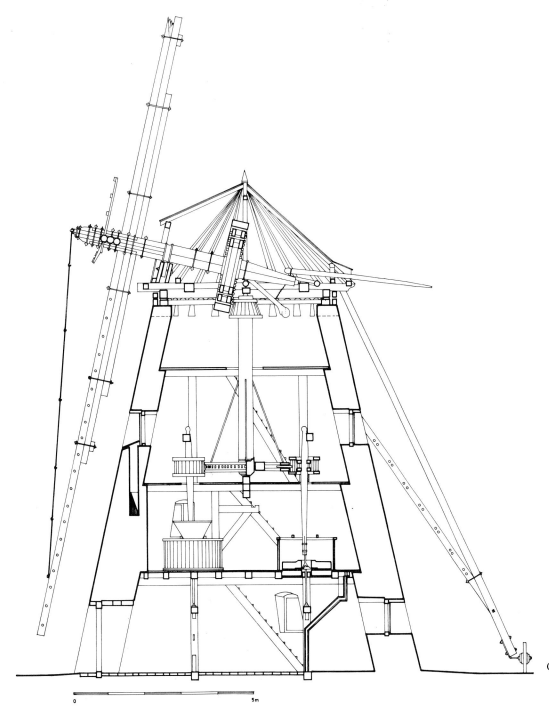

Cross-section of the Dusnok windmill

0   5m

35

a picture of the outskirts of a market town. The building has more than one floor and a cellar. The ground floor is divided into two major parts: there are the so-called beam-house and the finishing department. The two attic floors *(padlásszint)* have retained their original character of storing and drying: this is where the skins were spread out. The structure of the two floors, with a row of shuttered ventilating windows on each side of the drying loft, was characteristic to tanneries.

(5) The *windmill from Dusnok* is four-storied. Part of the ground floor is occupied by the miller's quarters consisting of a room and a kitchen with an open chimney. Near in the reception area *(fogadótér)*, are located the devices for adjusting the millstones. This was where the flour, cascading down, was received, and from here the grain to be ground was pulled up to the second floor. The grinding mechanism of the over-head drive type of mill with two pairs of stones is on the second floor; the gear transmission, consisting of the multiplier gear with the two rotating spindles *(pörgő orsó)* which can be disconnected as required, are on the third. The fourth floor contains the roofing timbers, the cogwheel which transfers the rotary movement from the wing boards to the main shaft of the mechanism *(szeles kerék)*, the axle common to the wing boards and the above cogwheel *(szeles tengely)*, the bevel wheel *(kúpos kerék)* and style *(bálvány)* as well as the turning mechanism and the braking device. The conical roof which can be rotated round the rim of the sheave is covered with shingles of pine wood. It is surmounted by the tin figure called "Rákóczi's horse", which rotated as the wind blew. The four wings of the sail, made of deal, were stiffened by iron rods hooked into each other. Canvas was stretched over the lathing of the wings. The roof was turned with the help of the turning wing of three beams and wheel travelling on the ground at the foot of the building.

The windmill will be re-erected on the farther-off, north-western fringe of the area representing a market town in the great Hungarian Plain where, with a detached farmstead and a vineyard nearby, the building density of the precincts will be made visible.

The regional unit representing Southern Transdanubia in the Open Air Museum will demonstrate the most typical characteristics of the vernacular architecture and interior decoration in the counties of Somogy, Tolna and Baranya and in the southern part of Zala county, as they developed in the economic and social circumstances of the 19th century.

Within the fairly large region, a number of lesser regions *(kistáj)* of ethnographic groups *(néprajzi csoport)* are pinpointed in the relevant literature, e.g. Sárköz, Ormánság, Belső-Somogy (Inner-Somogy), Zselicség, Szigetvidék, Drávaszög. The people of the eastern part and, to a certain extent, those living along the river Dráva, joined the national division of labour before the rest and, taking advantage of the booms in grain prices, became rich, and their art flourished. They were also quicker in embracing urban influences than the more closed, more conservative parts (Belső-Somogy, Zselicség, Muramente) in whose material culture many elements dating back as far as the Middle Ages have been preserved.

Each of the various local cultures embodied by the different buildings will show another stage of development. The fact that Southern Transdanubia is considered as one region is warranted by the common dwelling house prototype, which shows many similarities to the so-called Central-Hungarian house *(alföldi ház)*, which was most common in the Great Hungarian Plain.

Forty-five structures will represent the various stages in the development of vernacular architecture in Southern Transdanubia and the various aspects of the traditional culture of its inhabitants. The work of re-erection has not yet begun (1985). The buildings will be grouped on eight crofts, which will form a regular street. At the same time the aggregate and divided forms of settlement that took shape after the 150 years of Turkish occupation of Hungary, will also be shown. When making plans for the museum "region", we kept in mind the state of rural settlements before the replanning of villages in the middle of the 19th century. One half of the main street of a village will be shown with ribbon plots behind the farmyard, joined on one side by the old part of the village with its aggregate centre. From the end of the museum village a road will lead to the cemetery and the barn-yards (Ill. 23), symbolizing the dividedness of the settlement. In conformity with historical traditions, mainly middle-sized farms of peasants owning about half of the unit of land held under villeinage will be shown, but we also plan to present the homesteads of a smallholder and rich peasant.

The following descriptions of buildings proceed from the aggregate nucleus of the older village towards the ribbon plots along the main street. In this way we can follow the development of folk architecture in the region.

The *house* chosen and already taken down in *Szenna* dates to the years around 1860. It comprises a room, kitchen, pantry, shed and porch. This building will typify the stage when, after erecting timber-framed wattle-walls on groundsills, and then "mud and stud" structures, people in Somogy switched over to building with rammed earth walls. The ground plan of the already erected dwelling house of beaten earth, its chimneyless kitchen and the "eyed" stove concave tiles *(szemeskályha)* in its room, heated from the kitchen, are the same features as those of the Szenna houses whose timber-frame still rested on groundsills and had walls reinforced with stakes ("mud and stud" wall). The roof timbering, the way of laying the roof and the porch with its wooden posts also resting on groundsills are similarly unchanged.

Building in wood according to the traditions of Zselic will be represented by the outbuildings on the same premises. The timber-framed, wattle-walled *granary* removed from *Zselickisfalud,* rests on groundsills. The pigsty originating in Szenna will be re-erected in its original state with grooved post and board walls. The structures in the courtyard follow one another in a row, and only the barn stands crosswise at the end, in its original place. The farmyard is encircled by a horizontally woven wattle fence.

Master plan for the regional unit representing Southern Transdanubia

1–1: dwelling house from Zengővárkony; 1–2: small stable from Zengővárkony; 1–3: barns with stable from Zengővárkony; 1–4: pigsty from Zengővárkony; 1–5: fence and gate from Zengővárkony; 1–6: well from Zengővárkony; 2–1: dwelling house from Fadd; 2–2: maize barn from Fadd; 2–3: barn and shed from Fadd; 2–4: fence and gate from Fadd; 3–1: dwelling house from Szenna; 3–2: haybarn and stable from Szenna; 3–3: grain barn from Zselickisfalud; 3–4: pigsty from Szenna; 3–5: "tub" well from Tarány; 3–6: fence from Szenna; 4–1: dwelling house from Csököly; 4–2: pantry, stable, barn and shed from Csököly; 4–3: fence and gate from Csököly; 5–1: dwelling house from Zádor; 5–2: barn with stable from Zádor; 5–3: storage chamber for grain from Piskó; 5–4: outer grain barn from Darány; 5–5: pigsty from Zádor; 5–6: fence with gate from Zádor; 6–1: dwelling house from Muraszemenye; 6–2: henhouse and pigsty from Letenye; 6–3: small stable from Letenye; 6–4: maize-leaf hive from Letenye; 6–5: barn with stable from Muraszemenye; 6–6: pantry from Muraszemenye; 6–7: dove-cotes from Felsőszemenye 7–1: dwelling house and outbuildings from Őcsény; 7–2: fence and gate from Őcsény; 7–3: draw well from Őcsény

8–1: dwelling house from Drávapalkonya; 8–2: stable from Drávapalkonya; 8–3: pigsty from Drávapalkonya; 8–4: maize barn and pigsty from Drávapalkonya; 8–5: well from Drávapalkonya; 8–6: fence and gate from Drávapalkonya; 9: belfry from Bodolyabér

The buildings removed from *Csököly* for the next croft exemplify the most archaic version of the timber-frame on groundsill form of architecture surviving up to now (Ill. 24) from Inner Somogy which is one of the areas in Southern Transdanubia where traditions have been most faithfully preserved. The farmhouse has a timber-frame on its groundsills and the gaps between the vertical posts of the frame are filled with mud. It consists of a room, kitchen and pantry, with a porch *(tornácbeugró)* taken from the front part of the kitchen. When taking down the house, we found in its chimneyless kitchen with an open hearth the remains of the once so popular wattle-walled oven made in the shape of a truncated pyramid and having a fire bench. Although the walls are topped with a raftered roof (there is only one ridge-pole roof in the area that we know of), its shape is traditional: both ends are fully hipped. At

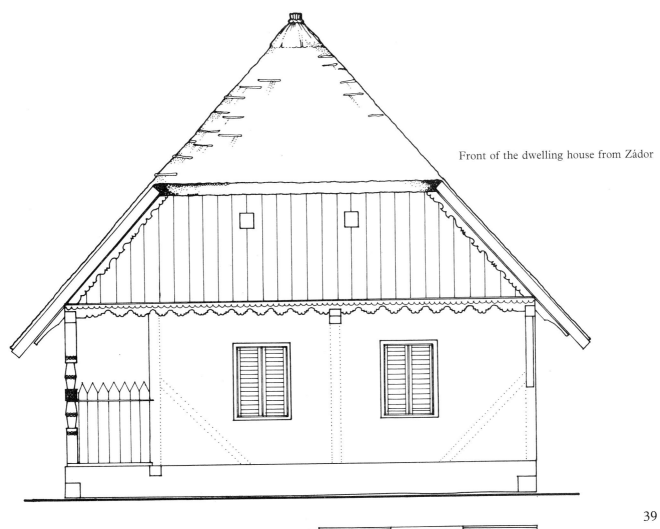

Front of the dwelling house from Zádor

0   3m

39

the time of taking the house down this was the only hipped roof in Csököly, but according to the evidence of photographs taken in the 1930s this shape of roof was once characteristic of the streetscape. The homestead portrays a small farmer's house and outbuilding in the area. Near the dwelling house, in the wider back part of the courtyard, the latter will be located, a timber-framed construction on groundsills, comprising *twin chambers (ikerkamra)* (press house and wine store), *stable, barn* and *shed.* In the street by the fence, a *bodonkút* ("tub well") used to stand whose 9 inch thick lining and brim are formed of a hollowed out oak trunk. It was commonly used by the inhabitants of the surrounding houses.

The buildings for the next plot are from the villages of a territory along the river Dráva where building in wood used to prevail. The *dwelling house* whose frame lies on

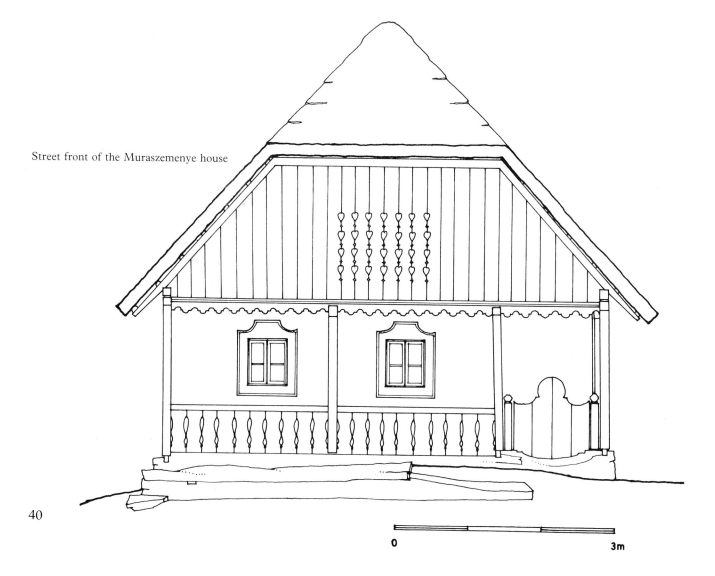

Street front of the Muraszemenye house

40

0   3m

Axonometric drawing of the Muraszemenye house

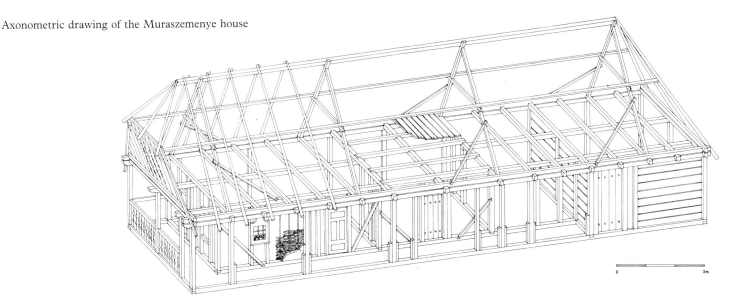

groundsills and whose cob wall is reinforced by stakes ("mud and stud"), was erected in 1860 in *Zádor*. Its raftered roof is half hipped *(csonkakontyos)* and its plank gable protrudes. It is worth mentioning that the main beam, which had supposedly been taken from an older house of two divisions *(kéthelyiséges)* when it was pulled down, is ornamented by fluted hollows. The arrangement of the house is room, kitchen and pantry. The kitchen is chimneyless, and originally held an Inner-Somogy, Zselic type of oven. The room was heated by an "eyed" stove with concave tiles. In our century the pantry was already used as a living room *(lakóhelyiség)*. The house will be put up again to look as it did when first erected.

The large *stable with barn* is a sign of numerous livestock. Cattle dealers of Zádor are mentioned in records from the end of the 18th century. The carefully executed *granary from Piskó*, was to store the increased amount of grain crops. An outfarm with a *grain barn* also belonged to the farm. A timber-framed *pigsty* of grooved post and board walls will also be re-erected in the courtyard.

The farmyard with the *house from Muraszemenye* (Ill. 25) represent a farm of medium size. This is the oldest, and the only wattle-walled building in this museum region; it was erected in 1833. It also exemplifies ridge-pole roofs which were formerly in common use over wide areas. Some of its elements show marks of the influence of architecture in western Hungary, especially the protruding carved and coloured, "falling forward" *(előrebukó)* gable. The arrangement of the house is room, kitchen, room and pantry, as was usual for a dwelling belonging to a serf tilling half of a unit of land held in villeinage, and accommodating an augmented family *(bővített család)*. The wooden porch is the oldest in the stock of structures that survives in Southern Transdanubia. The chimneyless kitchen has stoke-holes in its cross-walls for heating the "eyed" tile stoves in the rooms. The pantry has grooved post and board walls of oak planks. The *stable with barn* standing crosswise at the end of the farmyard dates to the second half of the 19th century. Its hardwood timber frame rests on groundsills and is topped by a ridge pole

Reconstruction of the street
front of the Őcsény dwelling house

roof supported by scissors beams *(ollószáras szelemenes tető)*. The barn part is wattle-walled, whereas the stable part has mud walls between stakes ("mud and stud"). The popularity of wattle work is shown by the *skep for holding maize (kukoricáskas)* (Ill. 22), the fence on two sides, and the low wattle fence surrounding the dung hill. The *fence between the courtyard and the street is made of planks.*

The *house* removed from *Fadd* (Tolna County) is an adobe construction of room–kitchen–room–pantry-stable arrangement, with a porch on the courtyard side. The front room is an unheatable "gala" room *(parádés szoba)*,

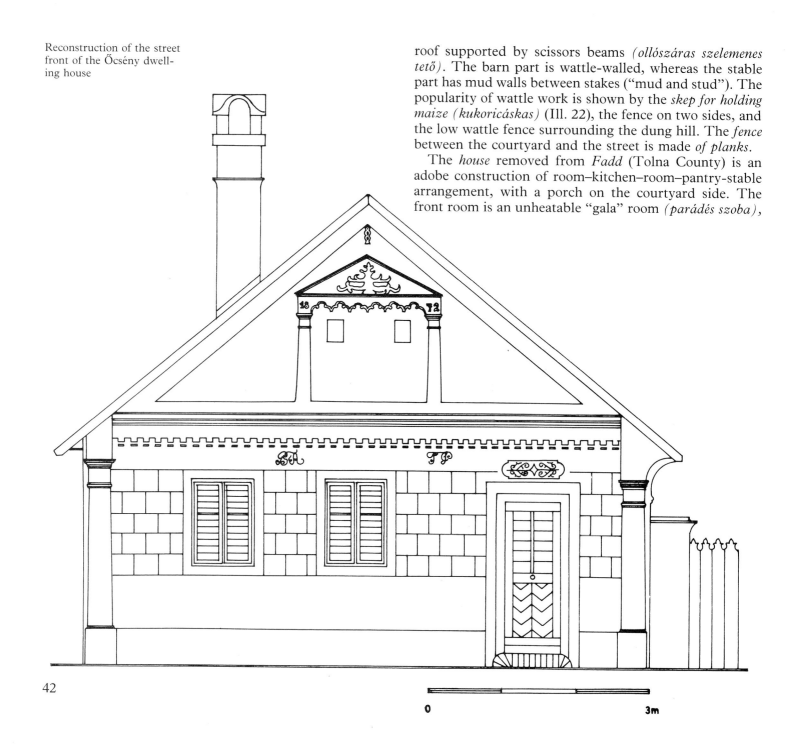

0   3m

whereas in the other room where the family actually lived was an oven in the shape of the frustum of a cone, type generally accepted in the Great Hungarian Plain, stoked from outside.

Smoke removal was done through an internally accessible flue (kamin)-type construction of increased cross section which stood in the kitchen. Over it the vault of a small open chimney, which served for smoking meat was erected in the attic. This exemplifies a transitional method of smoke removal, making use of elements from both open and closed smoke outlets. Furnishing the house will offer a splendid opportunity for giving a picture of the furniture makers' industry that flourished in Fadd.

On the other side of the street in the museum, buildings from Őcsény, erected in the 1870s at a time of economic boom in the Sárköz, will present the material culture of this ethnographical group at the rich farmer's level. The double *dwelling house* with cob walls was erected in the middle of the 19th century and consisted of a room and kitchen, then of a room, kitchen and stable under the same roof. Each room was heated by a glazed tile "eyed" stove of concave tiles, *szemeskályha* stoked from the neighbouring kitchen which had an open chimney. The house was rebuilt in 1872. It was then that the street front, documented at the time of taking it down, was made. In the course of taking the house down, three hollows which had been made for ovens, were found in the walls, with ledges for the fire, and two stokeholes for the "eyed" stoves.

In the lowermost layer of limewash on Neo-Classic fancy plaster work over the street front, we found a red and blue coating and the date 1872. The same date and initials, and the owners' names were found on one of the small, built-in wall cabinets and on a corner bench respectively. The roof construction in 1872 was already adapted for the room, kitchen, room, kitchen, pantry and stable arrangement. When re-erecting the house in the museum it will be restored to this state, with an open chimney and with an "eyed" stove of concave tiles in each room. The covered *chamber with carriage passage (kocsiátjáró-kamra)*, erected under the same roof in 1872, stood at right angles to the house, thus dividing the courtyard into two. Behind the first courtyard there was a backyard, surrounded by farm buildings, later constructions for storage needed by the rich peasant pursuing intensive farming: *barn, maize shed, cart shed, pantry and pigsty.*

An outsteading in the fields with three buildings also belonged to the farm, as well as a vineyard where a wine press house and pit cellar *(lyukpince)*, and a small house consisting of room, kitchen and stable arrangement stood as early as 1860.

The way people lived in the Drávaszél during the second half of the 19th century will be demonstrated by the *dwelling house from Drávapalkonya* (Plate XIV) and its dependencies. In contrast to the house from Zádor, this represents more urbanized forms of farming and interior decoration. The L-shaped adobe building with a cellar underneath has a ground plan of room, room, kitchen, pantry, summer kitchen *(nyári konyha)*, and stable-barn, with the rooms facing the street. Houses of cob and adobe walls were erected in larger numbers only after the flood in 1827. There is a collared roof and the double floor is covered with planks. The kitchen is warm because its ceiling is also plastered from below. The barrel vaulted open chimney, built of adobe, stands in the summer kitchen over a flat, angular oven. Every place in the house has a dirt floor. The croft of "one and a half inheritances" is so wide that a waggon could turn around the *sweep-pole well* in the middle. This central place is almost completely surrounded by buildings. The only open space on the side of the kitchen garden is enclosed by a *fence*. The timber framed *pigsty*, is a characteristic example of old pig-pens.

Animal husbandry played an important role in the life of Drávapalkonya. Besides keeping pigs and cattle, they also bred horses. This accounts for the fact that a farm of 12 holds (1,6 hectares) could support such a dwelling house and so many outbuildings.

At the end of the road leading out of the museum unit representing southern Transdanubia, the *belfry from Bodolyabér* will be re-erected. Its conical shingle roof is supported by Y-shaped wooden uprights.

The section representing Central Transdanubia or, by its other name, the Bakony–Balaton-felvidék (Bakony–Balaton Uplands), will mainly show vernacular architecture in stone. Stone structures predominate in the semi-circle which could be drawn by connecting Keszthely, Sümeg, Magyarpolány, Fenyőfő, Várpalota, Balatonalmádi and the Lake Balaton. Even neighbouring territories are characterized by mud-walled buildings. The fact that stone has been an easily available building material also indicates that this is an area of special ecological conditions whose economic and social development has been different from that of the flatlands that surround it.

From the two parts of the region, circumstances are more extreme in the Bakony. Fertile, loess-covered valleys alternate with barren karstic plateaux. As the cool climate and short growing period have not been favourable for grain production, forestry gained importance. The woods were also utilized in earlier centuries by grazing and as a source for mast.

The picture is different on the southern slopes of the Upland north of Lake Balaton (Balaton-felvidék). The equalizing effect of the Lake on the climate lends Mediterranean features to the area. In the eastern part there are many Permian red sandstone soils whereas basalt and basaltic tufa can more often be found in the fields lying west of Tihany. Such stones could, of course, be quarried on the fringes of the village for building purposes. Natural conditions were not favourable for the growing of corn crops in the Balaton-felvidék either. In the villages surrounded by a narrow area of fields there was also a scarcity of pastures. On the slopes of red sandstone and basaltic detritus, however, a flourishing culture of grape and fruit growing has developed. In the valleys and basins and the hilly and flat countries girding the uplands, especially in the vicinity of Pápa and Devecser, conditions were already favourable for both corn production and animal husbandry.

The two parts of the region also differ in respect of their historic and social development. As a result of the system of possessions in the early Middle Ages there were many villages here of noble legal status and the proportion of noblemen owning not more than one "plot" (unit of land held by a serf in villeinage) was higher than the national average. During the Turkish occupation of Hungary this was where the line of border castles ran and the campaigns and skirmishes thinned out the population. Whilst in the Balaton-felvidék the network of medieval settlements stayed close, in the greater part of the Bakony scarcely one or two villages were able to survive the holocaust here and there. To repopulate the devastated areas Hungarian, Slovak and, most numerous of all, German settlers arrived in several waves during the 18th century.

In the period of renascence following the Turkish occupation, the region showed a most variegated picture in both social and ethnic as well as religious respects. While the majority of the indigenous inhabitants, especially the lesser nobility, had embraced the Protestant faith, Catholics settled on the estates of the Church and in the villages of the new big landowners who were loyal to the Viennese Court. Sectarian strife, too, contributed to the fact that people of different ethnic origins settled in separate villages or parts of a village. The difference is obvious at first sight between the new settlements with their large, regular plots and broad streets, and the old, overcrowded villages of medieval origin with their confined centre.

The greater part of the territory in the region was either church land or belonged to the estates of large landowners. The numerical proportion of noble smallholders and curial noblemen *(kuriális nemesek)* tilling one "serf's plot" or part of one, although insignificant as regards the size of the estates or the number of serf's farmsteads *(jobbágyporták)*, continued to be high. Their way of life and methods of farming in most cases did not differ from those of the serfs. The overwhelming majority of serfs lived on a half or a quarter of a unit of land held under villeinage. An insignificant minority of the serfs held a whole unit of land whereas the number of cotters owning only a house or not even the roof over their head was about the same as that of the serfs with land to live on..

In the Balaton-felvidék grape-growing compensated the peasants for the few and poor fields and pastures. On the hills planted with vines, cellars of various sizes and forms of construction, possessed by local people and the inhabitants of other places, serfs and big landowners, church institutions and burghers followed one after the other. The cellar and its associated equipment in the vineyard were sometimes estimated to be of higher value than the whole dwelling house and farmyard in the village. In the vicinity of Alsóörs and the Kál Basin where sandstone fit for dressing was quarried, stone-cutting was a separate branch of industry (e.g. Kővágóörs [the name of a village in which Kővágó means stone-cutter]).

The differences of production between the two parts of the region made it necessary for the villages to be in trading contact with each other. An intensive exchange of goods took place in the busy market towns of Central Transdanubia. Under the conditions of lively interchange of products, cartage was an important source of income. A significant stratum of craftsmen lived in the market towns. Many of them (fullers, szűr-makers [szűr = long embroidered felt cloak of Hungarian shepherds], makers of wooden wine-canteens [csutorások], cobblers, tanners, cartwrights) were famous even beyond the boundaries of the county. The water power of the many brooks was utilized by countless flour, fulling and sawmills. There were even some early factories, established in the first half of the 19th century, operating like the potteries in Pápa and Városlőd, or the porcelain factory, which has achieved world fame since then, in Herend.

While a major part of the Bakony was covered by forests, building in wood was more widespread. Some 18th century records also mention wattle-walled structures. In the northern part of the Bakony and on its fringes bordering on the flatland, mud walls were the most common, whereas in the southern parts and in the Balaton-felvidék stone houses dominated.

The use of stone for architectural purposes became general in the 18th and 19th centuries, although in Central Transdanubia it has a tradition going back to the late Middle Ages. It was then that deforestation assumed such threatening proportions that a succession of laws and statutes resulted, to protect the woods. Building in stone gained ground mainly in those territories where, as far as we know, timber-framed and wattle-walled houses had been erected earlier. The squires, too, were in favour of the idea of constructing buildings of lasting materials. An important role may also have been played by the efforts of the lesser nobles, who wished to emphasize at least as regards house and interior decoration that their social standing was higher than that of the peasants. The houses with vaulted rooms often bearing a date and initials, built by the lower gentry, certainly required a mason's participation. We have data from the end of the 18th century on the guilds of masons and stone-carvers, often founded together with those of carpenters and tilers. Most of the badges of these guilds bore inscriptions in German. Masons also operated in the villages.

Another type of stone building with rubble walls laid in mud and ceilings of oak planks then, later, boards, could also be found on the crofts of the poorest serfs. The experience gained by a serf who participated in building work for the landowner on his days of socage service, or of village specialists, could have been enough for erecting such a house. Building in stone became usual in the vineyards perhaps earlier than in the villages.

The use of stone had its effect on the structure of the house. In earlier times the stone wall quite often reached eaves-level all round and the gable was made of boards, some of thatch or wattle, or was simply left open. In the period under review the gable wall, too, was increasingly built of stone to its full height and, from the middle of the last century, decorated with increasing frequency with patterns in plaster (vakolatarchitektúra). Stone gable walls, of course, did away with the need for scissors beams to retain the ridge pole. In the Kál Basin, for example, it was the gable walls which usually supported the ridge pole. The replacement of certain elements of the roofing timbers with stone walls also made possible an increase in the size of the buildings.

Dwelling houses here have had, since the late Middle Ages, three or more divisions. The chimneyless house, with a single heatable living space serving as both kitchen and room, is known only through archaeological excavations of the remains of late medieval villages. Side by side with them, as early as the Middle Ages, appeared houses of solid materials with rooms free of smoke and heated by "eyed" tile stoves which could be stoked from outside. Such houses, owned in all probability by members of the lower gentry, can be considered the forerunners of rural houses in the 18th–19th centuries. A still standing example of the late medieval village dwelling houses of the lesser nobility is the mansion in Alsóörs, which exhibits Gothic elements.

Chimneyless kitchens with an open hearth were universally accepted in Central Transdanubia, where even the smoke of the stove in the room escaped into the kitchen. This accounts for the fact that each division in the house had its separate entrance from an open veranda which gave some protection from the weather to the indwellers going from one to the other. Houses where the kitchen had an open chimney appeared in the 18th century and became dominant by the end of the 19th. From the very end of the last century, kitchens with closed, internally accessible

Master plan for the regional unit representing Central Transdanubia
1–1: dwelling house from Mindszentkálla; 1–2: pigsty from Mindszentkálla; 1–3: apiary from Mindszentkálla; 1–4: well from Mindszentkálla; 2–1: dwelling house from Kádárta; 2-2: pigsty from Kádárta; 2–3: apiary from Kádárta; 2–4: wooden pigsty from Kádárta; 3–1: dwelling house from Szentgál; 3–2: pantry, stable and barn from Szentgál; 3–3: well from Szentgál; 3–4: pigsty from Szentgál; 3–5: gate from Szentgál; 4–1: dwelling house from Nyírád; 4–2: barn from Padragkút; 5: oil mill from Szentjakabfa; 6: water mill from Nyírád; 7: arched stone bridge; 8: common well; 9: roadside crucifix; 10: Catholic chapel; 11: Catholic cemetery; 12, 13 and 14: press-houses with cellar from the Balaton-felvidék

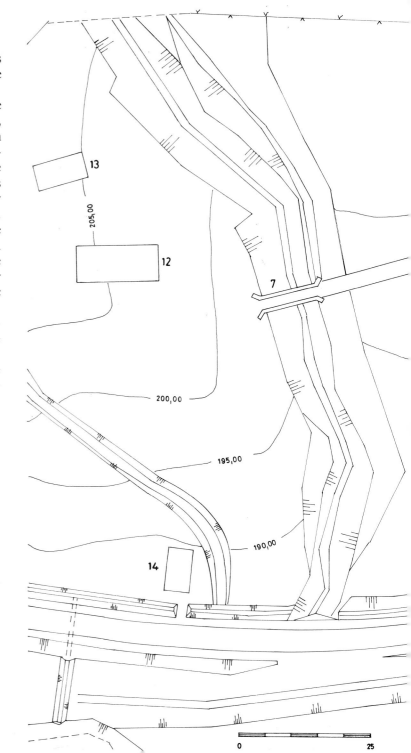

flues have become widespread, with cooking taking place on the cooking range. As they appeared, the "eyed" tile stoves stoked from outside were replaced by tile and iron stoves whose fire was fed in the room where they stood.

In most cases the farm buildings stand in a row on the croft. The dwelling house is followed by the stable and then the barn, with only a pigsty located opposite them (Ill. 26). On the other hand, the row of barns standing crosswise and closing the ends of the farmyards has been a characteristic feature of German villages (where the descendants of German settlers live). The small pots of irregular form and the variegated features of the terrain resulted in different courtyard layouts from which out-buildings were often missing. On the other hand a press-house with cellar, often completed with a room, located in the vineyard on one of the hills, also belonged to the farm.

The way of life of people in Central Transdanubia will be presented in four farmyards which also exemplify the characteristics of building in stone. The regional unit will be completed by two mills, three vineyard structures, a Catholic Calvary and cemetery, arched stone bridges, a roadside crucifix and a public well.

The houses will be sited in the street in herringbone fashion. Three crofts will lie on the left side of the street, whereas the fourth will show its back as if there was a parting of the way. This pattern was usual both in medieval settlements and in villages established in the 18th century.

The first *house* on the left has come from *Mindszentkálla* (Ill. 27). It used to stand in the courtyard of a small farmer who owned 3 or 4 holds (approx. 1.5–2 hectares), most of which was under grapes. The building of room–kitchen–stable–shed ground plan, with chimneyless kitchen, was probably erected in the middle of the 19th century and has reached its present form after several additions and altera-tions. It represents the stone architecture of the Kál Basin in its mature form. The posts and arches of its protected entrance *(gádor)* were also laid on flat stones. The ridge pole was supported by the stone gable walls and the pillar that reached into the loft. The unusually spacious kitchen

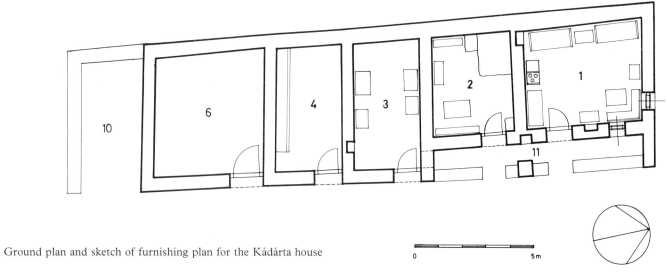

Ground plan and sketch of furnishing plan for the Kádárta house

0   5 m

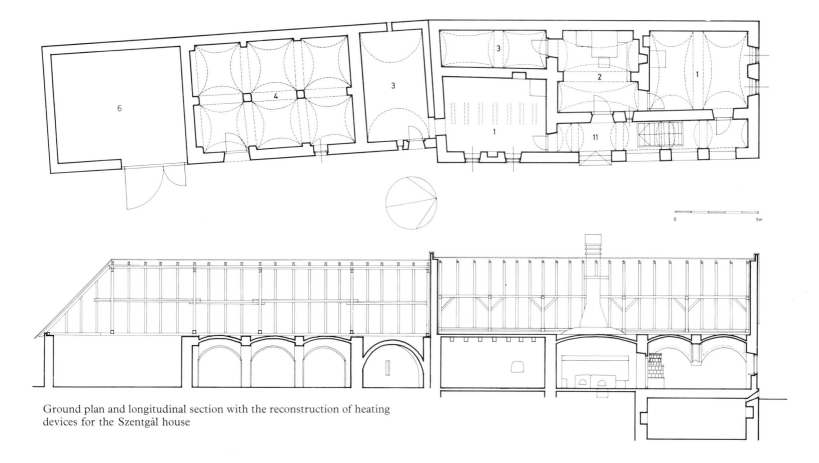

Ground plan and longitudinal section with the reconstruction of heating devices for the Szentgál house

also served as a pantry. A stone apiary and pigsty, and a well also belonged to the farmstead.

The next building on the left side of the street is the cotter's house from *Kádárta*. The structure of chimney-less kitchen and thatched roof was erected in the earlier half of the last century in two stages. The room and kitchen with the veranda, ceiled to provide a loft and running along one side and supported by stout posts, were followed a little later by the pantry, stable, barn and a lean-to shed. The roofing timbers, which have been repaired several times, show more than one form of support for the

ridge pole. The ends of the ridge pole rest on the gable walls, and there are scissors beams and Y-shaped uprights on the cross walls in between to give further support. An *apiary* and a *pigsty*, both built of stone, and another *pigsty* with wooden side-walls, complete the group.

The Kádárta house was inhabited by the descendants of cotters who owned 2 holds of land at the turn of the century. The head of the family augmented his income by working also as a day-labourer and by pursuing home crafts from time to time. To this day, the room has preser-

49

ved its original arrangement and also used in it were items of furniture dating from the first half of the 19th century (Plate XV). This is why one of the branches of the domestic woodworking industry, characteristic of the region, will be presented here: in the former part of the pantry a handle-maker's workshop will be fitted up.

The most distinguished group of buildings, the *dwelling house from Szentgál* and its *outbuildings*, will lie behind the Kádárta croft. The inhabitants of the village, as the king's hunters, had enjoyed the privileges of nobility since the Middle Ages. The Protestant owners of this house also belonged to the lower gentry. Besides a farm of over sixty holds (34 hectares), they also had wooded property and a vineyard in the Balaton-felvidék.

The first room is covered by a groined vault divided into two by an arch. A barrel vaulted cellar runs beneath, accessible by way of steps from the porch. The back room with its plank ceiling has a vaulted chamber behind it opening from the kitchen under the chimney; this marks the initial stage in the development of the house into a two-winged arrangement. The stone of the walls and the bricks of the vaulting were both laid in lime mortar. The queen post roof is covered with plain tiles.

The farm building, constructed as a continuation of the dwelling house, was made by using even more sophisticated techniques of vaulting. The back part of the barrel vaulted chamber was occupied by built-in partitioned granaries. The stable is divided by two central columns, and by arches, into six parts, each covered by a groined vault. It could house a large quantity of livestock.

The furniture will reflect a stage around the turn of the century, with hardwood furnishings, china bowls and cups made in Herend, and oleographs on patriotic subjects on the walls, indicating a taste associated with a bourgeois outlook (Plate XVI).

The structures of the farmstead on the other side of the street have come from a plot of land in *Nyirád*. The *farmhouse* is the earliest building in the regional unit. The main beam in its kitchen bears the following inscription: "Nagy György Mihály és Márton fiaival építette Melyben

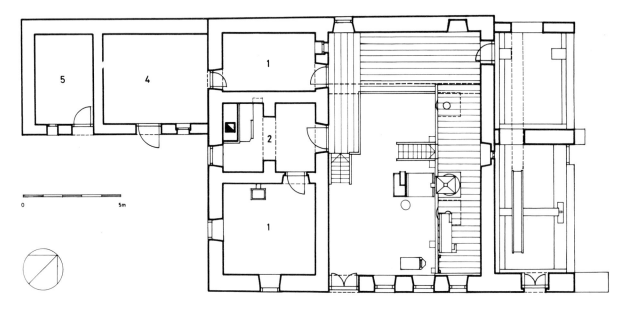

Water mill from Nyirád (state at the time of dismantling with structural reconstructions)

az Úr Jézus ditsértessék Ámen 1754" (Built by György Nagy and his sons Mihály and Márton for which the name of Lord Jesus be praised Amen 1754). In continuation of the house which had a ground plan of room, kitchen, pantry and stable, one of the brothers, who was making himself independent, erected a second dwelling house in the common courtyard around 1780. (It was demolished a few years ago.) It was very probably then that the *twin barns* standing crosswise at the end of the farmyard were set up for the two brothers.

The first three divisions of the house open on to an open porch *(gádor)* without a parapet. The tops of the stout pillars of the porch are connected with arches to the courtyard front, forming something like a row of flying buttresses. Porches of such a form are characteristic of the folk architecture of the Balaton-felvidék. The unnecessarily thick pillars most probably result from the technique of walling; that is, the stones were seldom dressed. The saddle roof with ridge pole on scissors beams is covered with thatch. The first, second and third rooms each have a main beam perpendicular to the longitudinal axis of the house.

The major branches of local industries, the factories and rural homecrafts will be represented by their products used in the village households. The modernization of agricultural implements, however, can only be perceived on the large farms.

The *oil-mill from Szentjakabfa* (Ill. 29), a Catholic German village, will be set up, in conformity with its original location, at a little distance from the buildings of the homestead, at the end of the Mindszentkálla croft. It is an outstanding relic not only on account of its age (on one of its pair of grindstones the date 1744 can be read and the figure 1862 on its big wheel indicates the time of its renovation) but also because of its multi-purpose equipment. In addition to the making of oil, hemp breaking and, with one pair of grindstones, even grain grinding were undertaken in the mill from time to time.

From the numerous water mills set up on the banks of the swiftly flowing mountain streams, the *Honi Mill in Nyirád* (Ills. 28, 30) has been chosen for transportation to the museum because the traditional grinding apparatus, used before the general acceptance of roller mills and lifts, can well be reconstructed in it. From the mill building, *malomház*, the miller could approach his home through a gallery with a carved and sawn parapet. A *stable* and *shed* also belonged to the *miller's dwelling*. In the museum the mill will be shown with one set of millstones; missing structural elements will be replaced by the equipment of a similar mill in Nagytevel.

At a small distance from the regional unit, on the hillside, three vineyard structures will present grape-processing and the storage of wine in the Balaton-felvidék. One of the archetypes will be well demonstrated by the vaulted cellar and press-house, erected in *Pécsely* in 1819.

This regional unit portrays the folk architecture and interior decoration of the Őrség (Vas County), as well as Göcsej and Hetés (Zala County). The buildings, transplanted from various parts of the two counties represent more than one version of the most characteristic building types of Western Transdanubia. They have been organized in clusters to recreate a village in its original environment, the form of settlement characteristic of the region. When planning the furnishing of the houses, our main consideration was the extent to which the individual objects reflected the most typical features of contemporary interior decoration.

As a consequence of their particular natural, economic and social circumstances, settlements along the southwestern border of Hungary preserved a form of settlement, architecture and style of interior decoration up to quite recent times that can be termed archaic, and can only be found in small patches elsewhere.

The hilly region of Vas and Zala Counties is an area of subalpine character, covered with forests and slashed by deep river valleys. Although these parts get most of the precipitation in the country, their soil is scarcely suitable for plant production. As late as the beginning of the 19th century, these hills were under huge oak– and beech-woods, although in the forest of the Őrség and Hetés, Scotch firs, too, can be found. Even in the middle of the last century, a subsistence economy was characteristic of this territory. The production of field crops was on a low level but hemp was grown in large quantities. Gathering of food had also retained some of its importance. Adverse natural conditions preserved until quite recently a form of animal husbandry based on grazing in clearings and high-level hay-making which, in turn, helped to shape the characteristically open and scattered form of settlements. Of the villages perched on hilltops or hiding in valleys, the *szeres* pattern of settlement—a group of hamlets under the same administration—is typical. Five to ten or more homesteads form a *szer*, and the majority of villages consist of five, seven or eight *szers*. Villages occupying less hilly areas are arranged in streets. The mode of covering a plot with buildings was, even in the latter half of the 19th century, what they called *kerített udvar* and *kerített ház*: the dwelling house, the storage room, pigsties, stables and even the barn, formed the sides of a square under a common thatched roof with the farmyard in the centre. There were houses sorrounding their courtyard on three sides only, and L-shaped, *hajlított* ("bent") houses, as well as examples in a straight line. In the last case, the outbuildings were freely scattered around the farmhouse.

The different forms of barns, with storage space *(kamrás pajta)*, stable *(istállós pajta)* and a protecting threshing floor ("throat" barn, *torkospajták*) are outstanding examples of building with hewn logs. These barns sometimes housed family festivities like wedding or christening celebrations.

The traditional peasant house in Zala and Vas Counties stood on a horizontal timber base (oak groundsills) and had walls of hewn fir or beech wood. The doors and

Master plan for the regional unit representing Western Transdanubia
1–1: dwelling house from Szalafő; 1–2: barn with chamber from Szalafő; 1–3: one-storied "kástu"
2–1: dwelling house from Szalafő; 2–2: barn with stable from Szalafő; 2–3: pigsty from Őriszentpéter; 2–4: draw-well from Szalafő; 3–1: dwelling house from Kondorfa; 3–2: well from Kondorfa
4: blacksmith's forge from Szentgyörgyvölgy
5: belfry from Felsőszenterzsébet
6–1: dwelling house from Baglad; 6–2: barn from Resznek; 6–3: sweep-pole well from Nemesnép; 7–1: dwelling house from Szentgyörgyvölgy; 7–2: apiary from Bajánsenye; 7–3: flax-drier from Magyarföld; 7–4: projecting threshing floor barn from Iklódbördöce; 7–5: Woodshed from Szalafő
8: dwelling house from Rédics; 9–1: dwelling house from Vöckönd; 9–2: barn from Padár; 9–3: pigsty from Egervölgy; 9–4: stable from Egyházashollós; 10: roadside crucifix from Lendvadedes; 11: village well from Rigyác; 12: pulley well from Szalafő; 13: press-house with cellar from Rédics; 14: press-house with cellar from Lendvadedes; 15: press-house with cellar from Kőszeg; 16: press-house with cellar from Letenye; 17: press-house with cellar from Bocfölde

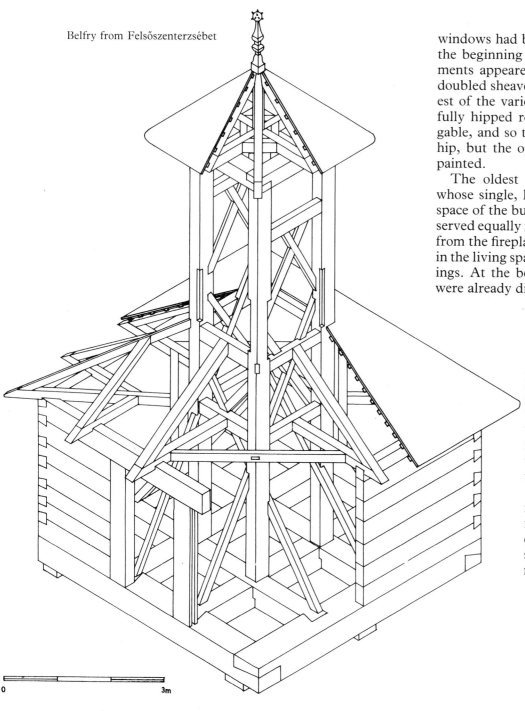

Belfry from Felsőszenterzsébet

0   3m

windows had been carved of oak until the last century, at the beginning of which carpenter-made doors and casements appeared. The roofs were covered by bound and doubled sheaves of thatch. The simplest and perhaps oldest of the varied roof shapes and front formations is the fully hipped roof. This was later truncated. At first the gable, and so the loft also, was open under the truncated hip, but the opening was later covered with planks and painted.

The oldest type of house is the chimneyless house, whose single, large, heatable room constituted the living space of the building. Its huge square oven, made of clay, served equally for heating, cooking and baking. The smoke from the fireplace and the mouth of the oven spread freely in the living space and escaped through the available openings. At the beginning of the 19th century such houses were already disappearing, being replaced by houses with a chimneyless kitchen and a smokeless room heated by a tile stove.

The majority of the inhabitants of the region were the descendants of frontier guards and so members of the lower nobility, whereas a smaller proportion lived in serfdom. The houses and interior design of the minor gentry, and the settlement pattern of their villages were, in almost every respect, identical with those of the nearby villages inhabited by serfs but belonging to the region.

The re-erection of buildings from this region has already started in the Szentendre Village Museum. Passing the roadside crucifix, the visitor arrives at the small square, the centre of the village, in the middle of which stands the shingle-roofed,

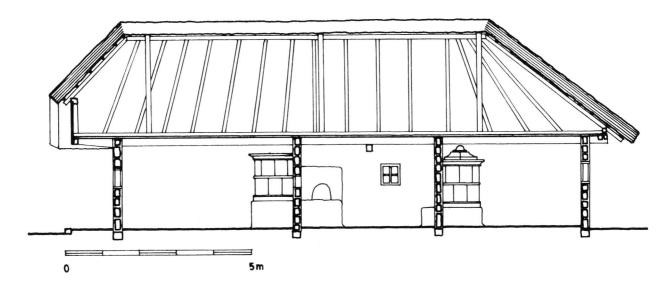

Longitudinal section of the Szentgyörgyvölgy house

log-walled belfry, originally erected in *Felsőszenterzsébet* around the end of the 18th century. Homesteads from Zala are grouped around the square.

First on the left side of the road is a poor peasant's *house from Vöckönd* (Ill. 32). The timber-framed building, whose daubed wattle-walls are reinforced with stakes, stands on hewn groundsills. Under the hipped roof there are three divisions. The chimneyless kitchen is served by an oven built of mud and the room is heated by a tile stove stoked from outside. Its furniture represents the interior decoration used by poor peasants at the end of the last century. In the courtyard a *pigsty* of cross-notched log walls made of hewn oak and a thatched roof, a wattle-walled *stable* and *bee-hive*, as well as a timber-framed barn, can be found. One of the outbuildings bearing the oldest date (1811) in the museum is the wattle-walled *protecting threshing floor barn from Egyházashollós*.

On the other side of the square is located the *Szent-györgyvölgy dwelling house* (Ill. 31 and Plate XVII) and farm buildings, a good representative of crofts owned by well-to-do peasants. The "bent" house of L-shaped ground plan was built of logs in the second half of the 19th century. The half-hipped roof is thatched. The kitchen is chimneyless but the two rooms are heated by a green stove of flat glazed tiles. The front room has been furnished with pieces of furniture dating from the last years of the 19th century, with objects characteristic of the taste of "middle peasants" developing bourgeois attitudes. The back room was used as a tavern at the turn of the century on the occasions of annual fairs, and has been furnished accordingly. The *protecting threshing floor barn from Iklódbör-döce* (Ill. 33) is one of the most expertly made log buildings in the territory. Opposite the kitchen of the L-shaped house stands the usual outbuilding of Őrség and Göcsej farmyards, a *woodshed from Szalafő*. A little farther from the dwelling house are two smaller farmbuildings: a little *structure for distilling spirits and drying flax from Magyar-föld* and the *apiary* transplanted from *Bajánsenye*, in which the skeps made of twined thatch stand in neat rows on benches.

The *dwelling house from Baglad* and the barn belonging to it will be erected behind the Felsőszenterzsébet belfry. (In Baglad, the house used to stand in a small square, behind a belfry.) It was built in the middle of the 19th century, of logs laid horizontally over the hewn oak groundsills. The wide, half-hipped roof, resting on a ridge pole supported by scissors beams, is covered by thatch. This type was common in the villages of Hetés and Göcsej, and was especially liked by well-to-do farmers. The one transferred from Baglad was one of the last of such structures. The pentagonal *barn from Resznek* will be one of the outstanding examples of log buildings from western Hungary. It was erected of hewn larch in the middle of the last century. Its roof covered by finely tied sheaves of thatch, the arched lintel over its huge two-leaved gateway and the projecting ends of the logs, all testify to the fine craftsmanship and developed technique of local carpenters. The barn will be shown decorated in readiness for a wedding party. On the Baglad croft a *sweep-pole well,* widely distributed in the lowland villages of Zala and Vas Counties, will also be set up. Such wells were usually owned by more than one family.

The *dwelling house* with carved gable, transferred from *Rédics,* was built in the second half of the 19th century. The half-hipped roof of the log-built chimneyless kitchen is covered with double sheaves of thatch. It represents a version characteristic of the Hetés area and its colourfully painted gable boards constitute an outstandingly attractive specimen of gables in Zala.

On the left side of the road, just opposite the house from Rédics, a later type of *dwelling house* is represented by the one from *Szalafő* (Ills. 34, 35). Both in its outside appearance and interior decoration it forms a transition from the traditional West Transdanubian folk architecture and furniture to the material culture of a more urban way of life in the early 20th century. The whitewashed brick walls, tiled roof and protruding porch as well as the furniture that reflects a petty bourgeois outlook are all typi-

Street elevation
of the Rédics house

0   2m

Longitudinal section
of the Rédics house

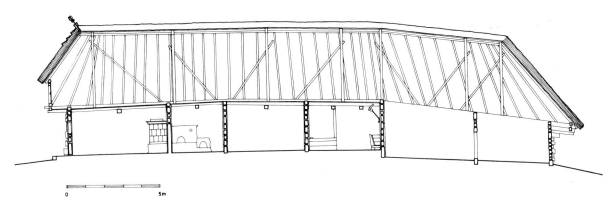

0   5m

cal of the period. A long whitewashed *stable* will be re-erected by the house. This stable, on supports of fired brick, and
built under the same roof as a barn of planks in the second
half of the 19th century, is a structure characteristic of the
peasant farms whose owners had switched over to stockbreeding on a large scale.

On the carved barge boards and on the main beam in the
room of the thatched *log house* transferred to the museum
from *Kondorfa,* inscriptions tell the year of its building:
1826. Since then it has been rebuilt more than once. Chim-

neyless kitchens were altered to kitchens with open chim-
neys, especially in the cases of schools, priests' and teachers'
houses. On the basis of the traditions of Kondorfa and other
villages in the Őrség, we wish to furnish a schoolroom, as
they looked in the latter half of the last century, in the room
of the dwelling house.

Proceeding on the road the visitor will pass the *smithy
from Szentgyörgyvölgy.* The log building with tiled roof,
preceded by a porch, erected at the end of the last century,
is now the only specimen in the territory covered by the

Ground plan
of the Kondorfa house

10   3   1   2   1

11

0   5m

museum of a wooden smithy. Tolls used by the poorer blacksmiths of the village at the turn of the century will be on show in it.

On the hill of vineyards belonging to the museum unit devoted to Western Transdanubia, various types of vineyard buildings will be re-erected. The one-roomed wine *cellar* of cross-headed log walls and half-hipped roof covered by thatch was erected by a Lukácsház vine-grower on the *Pogányi Hill near Kőszeg* in 1874. The most widespread type was the two-division press-house with cellar, like the one removed from the *Belső Hegy in Bocfa*. The *twin cellars from Letenye* is a structure divided into three

parts. It held the wine of two families, both of which used the press. The lintel of the log building with its dovetailed joints bears the inscribed date: 1840. In the press house is a large-sized beam-press with "basin" (a wooden trough). Yet another type will be represented by the *vineyard building* of four "waists" (room, presshouse, cellar and shed) to be removed from *Petőmihályfa* which also served periodically as a dwelling place.

From the row of cellars the road leads to the croft from the Őrség *szer*, the buildings surrounding a farmyard from Szalafő. Not more than two specimens remain of this traditional *kerített ház* of archaic technique: one is on its

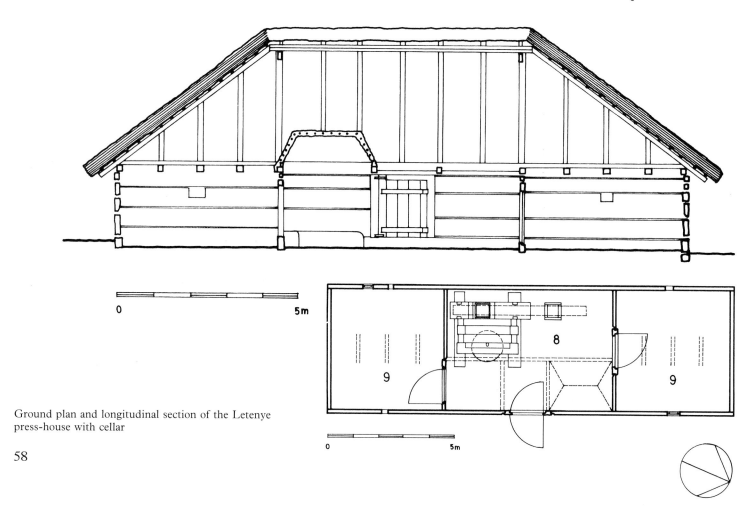

Ground plan and longitudinal section of the Letenye press-house with cellar

0   5m

0   5m

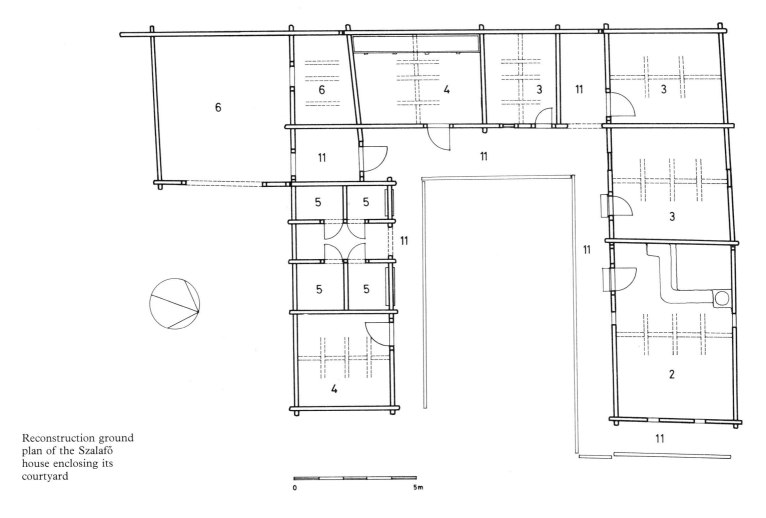

Reconstruction ground
plan of the Szalafő
house enclosing its
courtyard

0   5m

original site (Pityer-*szer*, Szalafő), and the other has been transferred to the Szentendre Open Air Museum. The log-walled building with its half-hipped, thatched roof, was most probably erected at the very beginning of the 19th century. The first, huge "room" was a chimneyless living space with a large-sized oven of clay. This is where the interior of an Őrség dwelling place, as it looked in the early years of the 19th century, can be shown. One of the proud possessions of our museum, a hewn bed from *Lendvadedes*, now a rarity, will be on view here with other pieces of furniture hewn and carved in the 18th century. A little farther from the dwelling house a storage room from *Szalafő* for both threshed and unthreshed grain will be set up. The one-floor *storage-chamber* for food *(kástu)*, which will be reconstructed on the basis of a survey made and a photo taken in 1940, will also stand by the road.

The buildings taken down and re-erected in the Museum represent the vernacular architecture of a territory much larger than the present Kisalföld (Little Plain, as against the Nagyalföld, the Great Hungarian Plain). The similarities of the material culture of this region, as well as the historical counties of Győr-Sopron, Moson and Komárom, to that of Csallóköz and Burgenland are readily perceptible.

The Plain in North-west Hungary was one of the important sites for the ancestors of present day Hungarians who conquered the Carpathian Basin in the last years of the 9th century. Ecclesiastical centres like Győr and Pannonhalma were soon formed. Since the western border-line was sparsely inhabited, in contradistinction to the densely set small villages in the eastern and central parts of the region, Germans were settled there in the 13th century. Communication roads along the northern and southern banks of the Danube favoured the development of through trade, in the wake of which the network of royal free boroughs (Győr, Sopron, Komárom), of towns producing agricultural goods and of market towns (Óvár, Kapuvár, Csorna, Csepreg) could take shape as early as the Middle Ages.

The Turkish armies marching against Vienna in 1529 and also smaller marauding companies burnt the villages down more than once. At the end of the 17th century it was the Croatian serfs settled by the lords of the big estates who, besides the Germans, constituted an important minority in the Kisalföld. At the turn of the 17th and 18th centuries, after a time of wars and counter-reformation, secular and ecclesiastical powers alike established manors (*majorságok*, farms managed by the landlord or his steward, where serfs worked on their days of socage) in the territories left masterless and uninhabited. In the early decades of the 18th century settlements of various sizes came into existence on the vineyard clad hills (Écs, Kisbaráti, Nagybaráti, Szemere, Sághegy). Most of the abandoned lands again fell into the hands of the owners of large estates, and formed the basis of further manors. The main

scenes of agricultural life were the plough-lands, pastures, hay fields and, in the hilly areas, the vineyards. In Szigetköz and Tóköz, fruit-growing and the production of sown vegetables were also important. Animal husbandry was only a sideline, especially in the villages of the Hanság, Moson, and Rábaköz. By the 18th century there remained few forests to supply the needs for timber and fuel-wood, so the important materials required for building were acquired in the neighbouring Austrian territories. Industrial production was primarily conducted in the work places processing agricultural produce. The most important role was played by the mills, above all water mills. Besides the guilds of mill owners *(malomtartók)* and millers, several coopers, weavers, tailors, wheelwrights, harness-makers, butchers, blacksmiths and cobblers worked in the villages. They usually pursued their crafts as an adjunct to agricultural activities.

Favourable natural conditions made it possible by the 19th century for some of the produce of the region, mainly wheat, to be regularly exported.

The high proportion of meadows and pastures resulted in significant stockbreeding. The hay grown here was purchased by Pozsony (today Bratislava in Czechoslovakia) and Vienna, but local cattle, horse and sheep-breeding were also based on it. On the estates of Magyaróvár, Nagycenk and Fertőd drains were dug, forests and orchards were planted and Swiss cows imported. Suitable machines from the Kühne machine works of Magyaróvár helped plant production, which had begun to develop anyway under the conditions of the corn boom.

Vernacular architecture in the Little Plain is characterized by the harmonious coexistence of archaic traditions, rooted in the Middle Ages but still living, with modern materials and developed techniques. Walls of mud, of unburnt "moorish" bricks and of mostly domestically made burnt bricks (which became widespread earlier here than in the rest of Hungary) are equally common. In some places a house or part of it (door and window-frames) was constructed of stone. Farm buildings were also built with wattle or reed-walls topped with reeds or, in some places, straw-thatched roofs, but burnt roof-tiles also appeared.

In the most archaic parts of the Plain in Northwestern Hungary (the Győr Basin and Sokoró) ridge-pole roofs supported by Y-shaped uprights visible from outside *(külső ágasos)* can still be found. On the other hand in the vicinity of Sopron, on the shores of Lake Fető (Lake of Neusiedl now in Hungary and Austria) or the Moson lowland area, roofs of king and queen posts respectively were constructed as early as the 19th century. The fact that stockbreeding made rapid strides at the turn of the century resulted in large stables and cow sheds. It was then that iron joists and cambered brick vaults *(poroszsüveg boltozat,* "Prussian cap vault" in Hungarian; *Stahlkappendecke* in German) became widely distributed in some places. The ceilings of the houses are dated and carved, sometimes with coloured open boarded double floors, and in some places with groined vaults raised of brick.

Two main types of heating and cooking installation can be found in the Kisalföld: an oven set up in the middle of the kitchen ("middle oven") was usual in the northwestern part of the region, and an oven located outside the back wall of the kitchen ("outshot oven"), in the eastern part. The heating of rooms shows even more variety.

The construction of the museum unit representing the Little Plain commenced in the early Seventies and was completed in 1988 (Ills. 37, 38; Plate XX).

The architecture of German villages around Sopron will be demonstrated by the replica of a house from *Magyarfalva* (Harka) and by farm buildings from its vicinity. On the shoe-lace patches characteristic elongated houses were built, as later structures were added to the existing ones. Three to five families lived on such a plot. Living quarters (room and kitchen) were followed by rooms fulfilling the functions of farm buildings. The walling of the domestic portion consisted of large-sized burnt bricks, the door and window-frames were carved of limestone and contained ornamented iron plates. Ceilings were either groined

vaults made of brick or open boarded double floors. In the kitchen with its open chimney stood the built-in cooking range with the cauldron-stand by its side; the "eyed" tile stove in the room was stoked from the fire-bench located sideways on in the kitchen.

The furniture shows the interior decoration used by poor German-speaking, Lutheran peasants and farmers of medium means who lived in the vicinity and so were, to a certain extent, under the influence of nearby towns like Sopron and Kismarton (Plate XVIII). In the room furnished in a traditional way with a corner bench there are two four-posterbeds *(Himlpet)*. On the top of the first a chest holding the funeral clothes *(todesz truja)* can be seen. On the wallshelf, hard earthenware *(keménycserép)* plates and jugs are arranged. On the walls are pictures of saints and of the adult male members of the family in uniform, a souvenir of the years they spent in military service. On the top of the four-posterbeds, short prayers painted or embroidered *(házi áldás)*, further devotional pictures and colourful china mugs, all tilted slightly forward, are visible. By the corner-bench stands a chest of drawers with glasses, china mugs and devotional objects on its top. The wardrobe is filled with clothes made at the turn of the century. On the arch dividing the kitchen space in two, colourful plates are hung, whereas on the back wall copper dishes and pottery can be seen (Plate XIX). In a small cupboard *(kaszni)* soup tureens and milk pots are kept. The dwelling rooms in the elongated house are followed by a pantry, then the *stable,* suitable for the livestock of three families, and finally the vaulted *wine cellar.* On the edge of the croft a *well* fitted out with pulleys, originally built in Fertőboz in 1869 and a *pigsty* stand. The farmyard is closed by two cross-passage *(áthajtós) barns* built of stone around 1860 in Fertőrákos and Balf.

The vernacular architecture and taste in interior decoration of better-off German-speaking inhabitants of the Moson plain are demonstrated by the replica of a *"double house"* built of burnt bricks in *Jánossomorja* (Mosonszentpéter). The two parts are connected by the common roof

61

Map of the regional unit representing the Kisalföld (Little Plain) 1–1: dwelling house from Süttör; 1–2: barn from Fertőhomok; 1–3: well from Fertőszéplak; 1–4: pigsty from Hegykő; 2–1: dwelling house from Bogyoszló; 2–2: stable from Bogyoszló; 2–3: barn from Rábaújfalu; 2–4: pigsty and hen-house from Bogyoszló; 2–5: well from Rábatamási; 2–6: wooden pigsty from Bogyoszló; 3–1: dwelling house and outbuilding from Mosonszentpéter; 3–2: built-in-well from Mosonszolnok; 4–1: dwelling house and outbuildings from Harka; 4–2: barn from Fertőrákos; 4–3: barn from Balf; 4–4: dove-cote from Harka; 4–5: well-house from Fertőboz; 4–6: pigsty from Ágfalva; 5–1: dwelling house from Ásvány; 5–2: barn from Kisbodak; 6–1: dwelling house from Rábcakapi; 6–2: barn from Rábcakapi; 6–3: well from Rábcakapi; 6–4: maize barn from Rábcakapi; 6–5: double pigsty from Rábcakapi; 8–1: dwelling house from Und; 8–2: barn from Horvátzsidány; 8–3: pigsty from Kiszsidány; 8–4: well from Und; 9–1: dwelling house from Táp; 9–2: barn from Táp; 9–3: well from Táp; 10: belfry from Alszopor; 11: statue of St. John of Nepomuk from Csepreg; 12: blacksmith's forge from Szilsárkány; 13: tread-mill from Mosonszentmiklós; 14: press-shed from Nyúl; 15: outside ovens from Kisbodak; 16: Calvary from Veszkény; 17: Votive chapel from Mosonszentjános; 18: Pieta from Veszkény

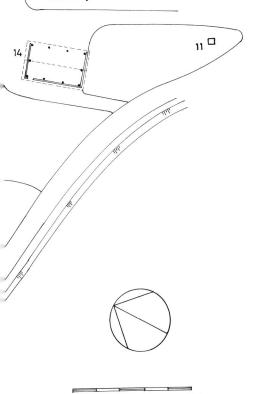

and gateway. The ground plan arrangement of the left one is room, kitchen, room, followed by a pantry, then a built-in *well* with pulleys (1849), after which the *stables* stand in a row. The right part comprises a room, a kitchen, then another room.

The right-hand kitchen has an open chimney under which, by the oven for baking bread, a cauldron-stand is visible. Both the tiled stove of the front room and the oven of the rear one can be stoked from the kitchen. The furniture with its dignified air formed the setting for the daily life of a Catholic German family. In the front room the corner-bench is placed where the wall running parallel with the street meets the rear one (Plate XXI) i.e., at the point where a small window had been cut. On the walls devotional pictures hang, along the longitudinal walls the beds and the wardrobe stand, and between the two street windows a chest of drawers can be seen. The furniture reflects winter conditions. The family lives in the back room where, besides the traditional pieces of furniture, the paraphernalia of embroidering, toys, and truckle beds *(Bettbank)* are also on display.

Vernacular architecture in the Rábaköz is represented by the *group of buildings* transplanted from *Bogyoszló*. The L-shaped archaic dwelling house, of a type appearing quite early in the Kisalföld, has a corridor in the middle. The walls of the so-called Megyesi house are built of locally burnt large-sized bricks. The ground plan of the longer left wing comprises room, kitchen, room, pantry and stables, whereas the shorter right wing includes a room, a pantry and a garret staircase and cellar steps. The house has rammed earth floors and timbered ceilings. The oven with a horse-shoe-shaped cooking place on top was set up in the middle of the back wall of the kitchen and is flanked by a cauldron-stand on both sides; each stand is followed by a fire bench under the stoke-hole of the tiled stove *(tábláskályha)* in the first room and the "eyed" stove in the back room (Plates XXII, XXIII). The furniture in the first room is arranged cornerwise. The surface of the table, standing in front of the corner-bench and in whose drawer bread was kept, is ornamented with marquetry.

63

There are two four-posterbeds by the back wall with a painted two-doored wardrobe (ómárium). In the chest from Komárom the clothes of the marriageable girl were kept and behind the door is a bed chest. The tiled stove was made in *Röjtök* in 1869.

The back room (Plate XXIV), where the young couple lived, savours of a more urban taste with its furniture of polished hardwood made by the local joiner. The furniture is arranged as it was when lunch had been brought in an attractive earthenware bowl, made especially for this pur-

pose *(komaszilke)*, to the woman in childbed lying in the four-posterbed curtained with a white cloth.

In the *room for storing corn (gabonáskamra)* a single-stone tread-mill dating from the end of the last century can be found by the built-in chests *(hombár)* made of fir wood. The *three stables* joining the domestic building, the wooden *pigsties (hidas)* in the courtyard and the huge *hay barn* with reed walls and roof mark animal husbandry on a large scale. The three-part barn was built in *Rábaújfalu* around 1860.

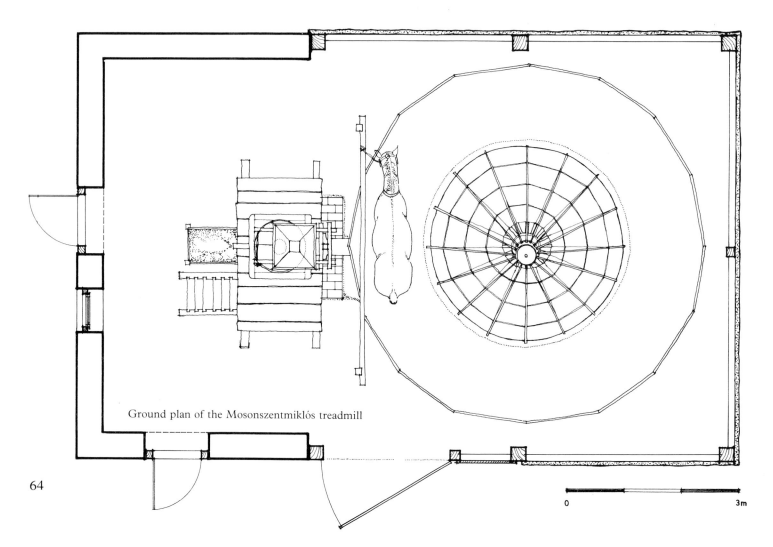

Ground plan of the Mosonszentmiklós treadmill

0   3m

The way of covering a croft with buildings arranged in herringbone fashion (Ill. 36), characteristic of the villages on the shores of Lake Fertő, will be shown by the *farmhouse* and its dependencies transported from *Süttőr* (recently made a part of Fertőd). The first section of the arched porch running along the courtyard front of the house and made of burnt brick, lies, as is typical of most village houses around the Lake Fertőd, in the street. The queen post raftered roof is covered with lugged tiles and its junction with the front is made harmonious by means of a cornice. In the niche at the front stands a painted stone statue of St. Florian.

The traditional exterior of the house conceals an interior, modernized at the beginning of the century. The first room has a soft wood planked floor and a flat plastered ceiling; this was one of the first ceiled rooms in the village. The kitchen (Ill. 40) was converted in 1914. The tall brick oven, built at the wall separating the kitchen from the first room, has a walled chimney with an internally accessible flue above. By its side there is a cooking range also made of brick. The furniture—made by the local joiner—in the first room presents the picture of a "clean room" *(tisztaszoba)* being influenced by bourgeois civilization. In the kitchen, iron and tin pans suitable for the cooking range, have replaced the earthenware pots. The back room is furnished in the traditional way with corner-bench (1871), four-posterbed (Plate XXV), a painted chest (1862) and a cradle. In the truckle bed *(tuli)* under the four-poster the bigger children slept. The back room was heated by a cast iron stove.

The huge stable of iron joists and cambered vaults consists of three units and is erected flush with the line formed by the posts of the porch. Opposite the house stands the *sweep-pole well*, with its pole *(kútágas)* carved and chiselled from oak, and its ancient stone curb dating from 1794. The croft is closed by a *barn* of deal walls standing on brick pillars. The two-part threshing barn was erected in *Fertőhomok* around 1860.

In the row of houses stands, on a separate fenced plot, the *tread-mill* transferred from *Mosonszentmiklós*. The

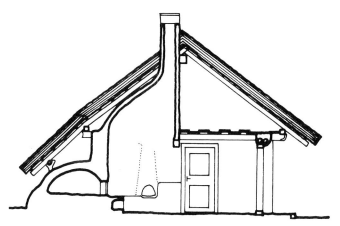

Ground plan and cross-section of the Táp house (working sketch)

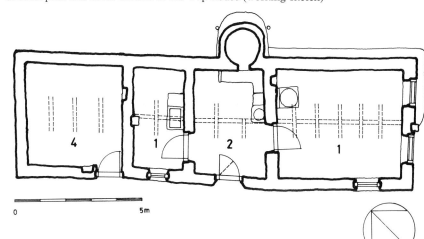

mill, operated by an animal marking time, is the only one of this type surviving in Hungary. Under the reed-covered saddle roof, the building is divided into a brick-walled milling house *(malomház)* and treading floor. As the inscription on the style *(bálványfa)* of the tread-wheel tells us, it was made in 1805. A pair of treading stones is situated on a stone bench *(őrlőasztal)* (Ill. 43).

The culture of the hilly countries of Sokoró and Pannonhalma are represented by the *dwelling house* and farm

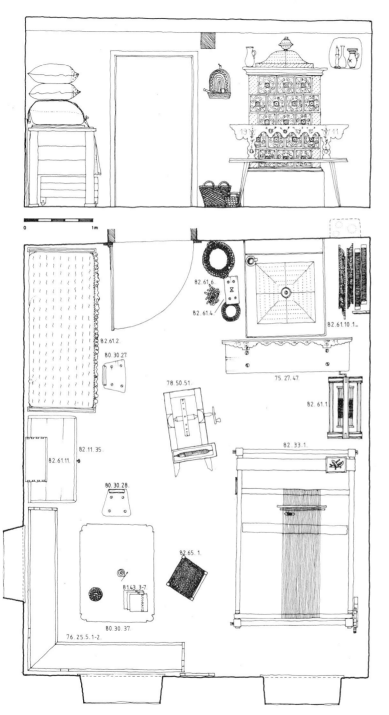

buildings removed from *Táp*. The house used to stand at the end of the village, on a plot irregularly cut out from the straight line of crofts by the road leading to the vineyard-covered hills, turning its back on the main road in a way characteristic of domestic buildings set up by cotters on plots allotted at the end of the 18th century. The cob-walled structure comprises room, kitchen, room and stable. The ridge-pole roof is supported by a Y-shaped upright standing in front of the short street front, and shorter ones standing on the cross-walls. The rooms have planked ceilings over the main beam. For the head of the family, who supplemented his income by weaving in the winter, a loom was set up in the room. The beds whose place it had taken were put into the pantry.

The back part of the kitchen is topped by an open chimney over the adobe ledges (Plate XXVI) for the fire. In the room there is an "eyed" stove of concave tiles, and the bread oven is on the outer side of the kitchen wall, as was usual in the Little Plain at the time. The mud-walled oven stands on a low bench, and is protected from rain-water by a lean-to continuation of the roof covering *(héjazat)*, supported on Y-shaped uprights.

The economic situation of the cotter family is indicated by the small size of certain farm buildings and the lack of others. The *stable* can house two animals. The *cart shed* is a simple plank-walled building, whose straw-stack roof is carried by Y-shaped uprights, just like the *pigsty*, or the *maize shed* made of split stakes. Its side could be raised or lowered, in accordance with the quantity of the crop and was topped by either straw or corn-stalks.

The material culture of the Croatian minority settled on the western border-line is represented by the *dwelling house* taken *from Und,* and the farm buildings taken down in neighbouring Croatian villages. The population of Und was mainly engaged in trading, cartage, dealing, basket-weaving and broom-making, besides tilling the land.

The cob-walls of the L-shaped house were raised in

Part of the furnishing plan for the Táp house (first room)

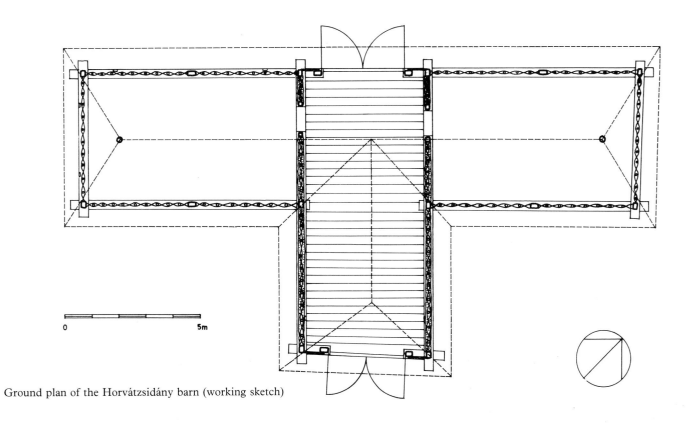

Ground plan of the Horvátzsidány barn (working sketch)

0   5m

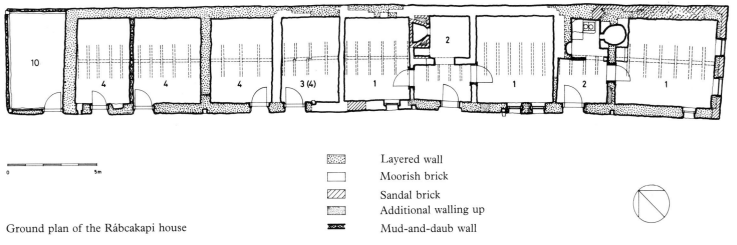

Ground plan of the Rábcakapi house

0   5m

	Layered wall
	Moorish brick
	Sandal brick
	Additional walling up
	Mud-and-daub wall

1841. Its longitudinal wing is of room–kitchen–room arrangement and in an unheated room of the cross wing, we have set up a basket-weaving shop. The kitchen in the longitudinal wing has an open chimney and the fine stove of the first room was stoked from here. The back room is followed by a pantry, then a stable. At the end of the croft the T-shaped *projecting threshold floor barn* stands crosswise; it was erected in *Horvátzsidány* in 1851. The timber-framed wattle-walled structure is topped with a thatched roof.

The earliest dated building of the regional unit in the museum is the *dwelling house from Rábcakapi* on the main beam of whose first room is the date: 1736. By the time it was taken down it had been altered more than once and comprised two dwellings, followed by four *stables* and a *shed*. The first dwelling consisted of a room and a kitchen, and its second room was later added to the second dwelling. Under the open chimney of the first kitchen, there is the stoke-hole of the "eyed" tile stove for heating the room, with a bench for the fire below. The bread oven projects beyond the kitchen wall. The second dwelling consists of a room, kitchen and another room, which earlier had been a pantry. On the cross beam of the left room the date 1863 can be read; it was then that the room received its present ceiling and was separated by a wall from the first dwelling. The rest of the building, the stables and the shed were put up before the 1880s. The kitchen in the second dwelling is also served by an open chimney over the brick-laid cooking range. On its right the stoke-hole of the tile stove in the room, and on its left the mouth of the prismatic oven, protruding into the back room, can be seen. The walling includes cob-walls, dried bricks and even wattle. The furniture and tools in the house are appropriate to a peasant farm whose owner lived off fishing and selling fodder besides keeping a sizeable quantity of livestock. At the end of the croft stands the large *threshing barn,* built around 1860 in *Rábcakapi*. Its raftered roof rests on oak posts; its sides are made of and its roof is covered by reeds, tied with withes.

The *belfry,* of rectangular ground plan, and of large-sized burnt bricks, stands in the middle of the village. The structure, used by people of the Lutheran faith, has been transplanted from *Újkér* (Alszopor). The bell, cast in 1855 to the order of the Monostor congregation, is held by the hewn pyramidal roofing.

The *Calvary from Veszkény,* dating from the end of the 19th century, occupies the mound by the road leading to the village and is surrounded by a low oak fence. On the three crosses and two posts the figures of Jesus Christ, Magdalene, Mary, John and the two thieves, cut out of tin plates and painted, can be seen. The statue of St. John of Nepomuk (Ill. 42) patron saint of roads, water-courses and bridges, was carved of limestone and taken to the museum from *Csepreg*. It also stands by the road.

The *smithy* transplanted from *Szilsárkány* is situated a bit farther from the houses, on the edge of the museum village. Its arched entrance, brick walling and groined-vault ceiling lead us to suppose that it was built on the basis or under the influence of manorial plans *(uradalmi tervek)* in 1812. Its equipment has been collected from the contents of more than one old blacksmith's shop. In the foreground of the workshop the device for bending and placing the wheel-bands on the cart wheels is set up. By the smithy, a lean-to shed for shoeing oxen has been located.

East of the museum street stands the *manorial press-shed and wine-press* with plank sides. The good quality white grapes and wines of the hilly region between the Bakony and the Győr Basin were also grown for sale. Some of the vineyards were in the hands of smallholders who organized themselves into vine-growing communities *(hegyközség)*. The Chapter of Győr and the Abbey of Pannonhalma also ran large estates. The tithe cellar and the huge *press* (Ill. 39) of the Győr Chapter were on the *Nyúl* (hare) Hill. As the inscription on the beam, of which one end is fixed and the other holds the screw and the weight, of the press (Baumpress in German), tells us, the structure standing on a solid stone pedestal was made in 1699 and renewed in 1852. As the original shed over the press fell into ruin, it has been reconstructed on the basis of old manorial plans.

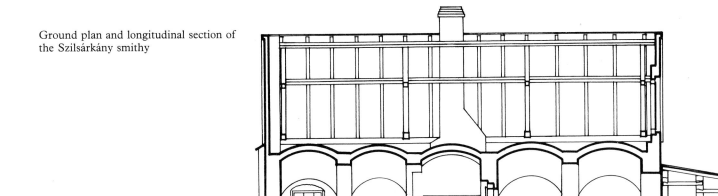

Ground plan and longitudinal section of the Szilsárkány smithy

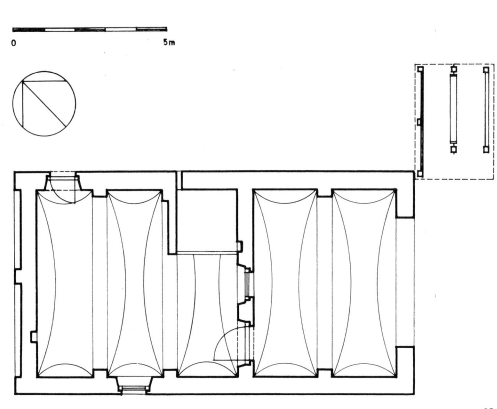

Around the press the implements for wine-treading, grape-crushing, pressing and the filtration of must are exhibited.

The votive chapel (Ill. 41) transplanted from *János-somorja* (Mosonszentjános) lies opposite the Szilsárkány forge. The brick building with a small belfry was erected after the cholera epidemic in 1842–44 from the contributions of the Roman Catholic German congregation for the veneration of St. Anne. Visitors can see the chapel, which was restored several times, and its furniture, as they looked in 1869. It is worthy of note that the more important motifs of the original murals were also saved.

The borders of the region are outlined by the market towns of Tokaj-hegyalja (Mád, Tokaj, Tolcsva, Sáros-patak, Sátoraljaújhely) on the one hand, and on the west by the rivers Sajó and Bódva, on the other. The western frontier, however, cannot be established quite unambiguously. In the development of dwelling houses no fundamental differences can be observed in northern Hungary up to the 16th century. Proceeding westward from the line of the river Ipoly, or perhaps even from that of the river Garam up to Ung, where the Hungarian linguistic area ended, three-division houses could be found. They were built of logs or had timber-framed and wattled walls topped by a rafter roof in the first case and perhaps by a ridge-pole roof supported by Y-shaped uprights in the second. In the room, which had no ceiling, there was a square oven surrounded by a ledge on which, in front of the oven-mouth which faced the windows, and open fireplace could be seen. The passage which gave access to the room and the pantry was also used for storage purposes.

The first changes occurred east of the river Sajó where smoke abatement in the living space took place in the 17th century. The house was only extended by a stable from time to time. No change ensued in the functions of the units. The pantry continued to serve for storage purposes and both walling and roofing stayed as they had been. What happened was that in the room appeared a smoke flue, *kabola* (Ill. 44), which collected the smoke issuing from the mouth of the oven and the open fire-place in front of it and channelled it through a slanting device above the body of the oven to the ceilingless passage *(pitvar)*. This was followed by two more alterations: first a ceiling appeared in the room, then an open chimney of wattle and daub over the back part of the passage. The latter was universally accepted from as early as the 18th century.

These features preceded by about a century the developments in the territories west of the river Sajó and their models can be sought in towns, market towns and among the houses of the minor gentry. It was, in all proba-bility, the welfare and prosperity at the beginning of the 17th century which resulted in the improvement of dwelling houses. The economic boom, however, proved short-lived and recession assumed disastrous proportions by the early years of the 18th century in the Hegyköz. This accounts for the phenomenon that houses preserving what were to all accounts and purposes early 18th century forms could be found in this area until recently.

Depopulation at the beginning of the 18th century had one more consequence: in the territory which had been populated almost exclusively by Hungarians, people of other nationalities appeared. According to regular plans, three waves of German settlers arrived between the 1730s and the 1790s; in the same century Slovaks and Carpatho-Ukrainians started to settle down in the Zemplén Mountains and in the Hegyköz (Abaúj county).

We do not intend to transplant buildings from the villages of German population and, in the case of Slovak and originally Carpatho-Ukrainian villages, e.g. Filkeháza, no difference can be traced in comparison with the surrounding Hungarian or German settlements. This is partly explained by the fact that the immigrants did not come from too far away, and had built similar houses where they originally lived. Those from the north were coming from territories where an earlier version of the dwelling house they found here was in use, so after settling down, development could be accepted with ease.

A characteristic form of settlement in north-eastern Hungary is the roadside village *(útifalu)* situated in a valley. The main street followed the course of a brook to

Master plan for the regional unit representing North-Eastern Hungary 1–1: dwelling house from Erdőhorváti; 1–2: barn from Fony; 2–1: dwelling house from Filkeháza; 2–2: barn from Füzérradvány; 2–3: apiary from Pusztafalu; 3–1: dwelling house from Nyíri; 3–2: barn from Nyíri; 4–1: dwelling house from Erdőhorváti; 4–2: stable from Erdőhorváti; 4–3: barn from Mogyoróska; 4–4: pigsty from Mogyorós-ka; 5–1: built and rock-hewn pit cellars

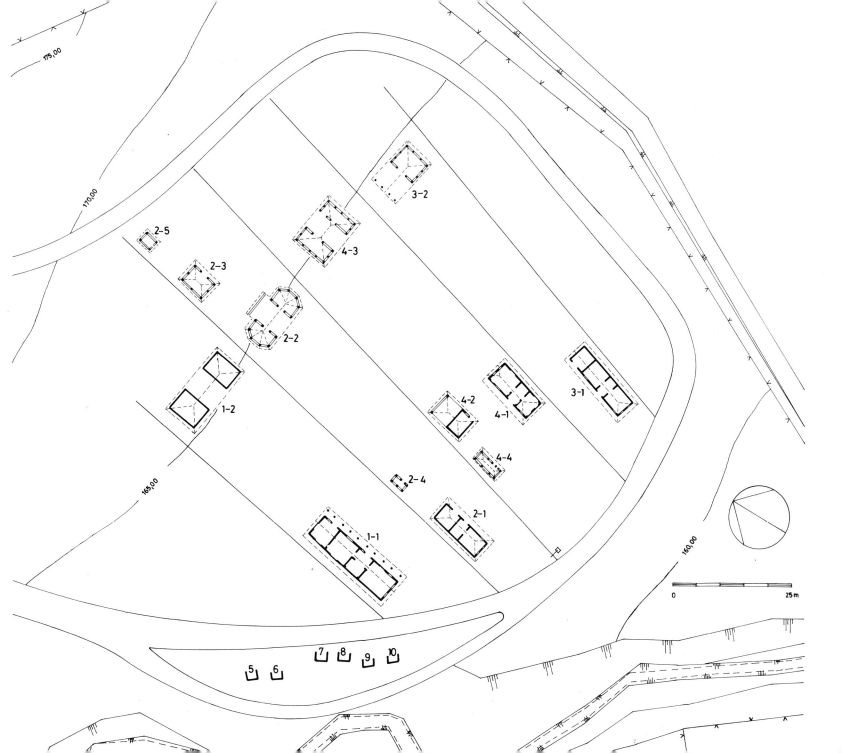

which the crofts, with structures forming a straight line or a line terminated by a barn standing crosswise, formed right angles. As small streams are usually not quite straight, the settlement and the shape of the plots often became irregular. The narrow farmyards, running uphill, are closed by barns stretching from edge to edge with an orchard behind containing perhaps a haybarn. There are, of course differences from place to place. In Mogyoróska, for example, some barns are not situated in the farmyard but opposite the house on the other side of the road. It could also happen that the barn was a continuation of the dwelling house and stable with only the threshing floor situated crosswise (e.g. in Komlóska). As the crofts run uphill there is a sizeable difference between the level of the street front and the end of the farmyard where the barn stands. The level of the front garden is, therefore, often raised as against the street and the house is erected on the terrace so created. There are places where this rise in level is done in such a way that the road, going along the rivulet, is flanked by cellars and the row of houses overlies the first constructed part of these cellars, as in Füzérradvány. It is this picture of settlement which we wish to show in the museum unit representing the region of north-eastern Hungary.

There will be four crofts at right angles to the street, above the cellars. Most of the structures have been transplanted from the former Abaúj and some of them from Zemplén county. The most archaic of them is the *log building from Filkeháza* which was most probably built in the earlier half of the 19th century (Plate XXIX). It comprises a room, a passage open to the roof and a pantry which used to be a stable. The passage gives access to the room, and the pantry has a separate entrance. When it was built, the house was typical of the homes of serfs living on medium-sized farms in the Hegyköz. Since then nothing but its heating has been altered. When the house was taken down, there was at the back of the passage, under the open chimney of daubed wattle, a large rectangular oven on a corner of which pointing towards the room, a small brick cooking range was erected. The wall between the room and

the back of the passage was, unlike the rest, of stone. This is where the mouth of the smoke flue belonging to the oven, stoked where it stood, remains.

Another important building on the croft is the *polygonal barn from Füzérradvány* (Ill. 50). The two-bay barn of octagonal ground plan and cross-headed log walls, whose shape is explained by the fact that it was erected of shorter logs, had a fairly wide distribution. Such structures occurred in Czecho-Moravian regions, the south of Poland, in the one-time Sáros county and northern Transylvania up to Zala on the west. It is planned that a *pigsty* and, in the garden behind the barn, a *haybarn* (Ill. 49) and an *apiary* (Plate XXVIII) will be set up on this plot. Following a model in *Komlóska* a *fruit-dryer* (Ill. 52) will also be reconstructed. This is simply a pit covered by a wickerwork skep on which the fruit was spread. Drying was speeded up by making a fire in the opening in the stone-lined mouth of the drying pit.

The buildings of the croft, next in chronological order, are all from *Nyíri* in the Hegyköz. The dwelling house in itself demonstrates all the changes in building construction and techniques that took place in this region. It also is an eloquent sign of the fact that wooden houses were not always considered immovable. The first unit of the house, the room, had originally stood in the neighbourhood of the church. At the end of the 19th century, two brothers inherited the house: one was left the room, and the other the kitchen and pantry. They then literally halved the house which was built entirely of wood in a technique between log-walling and making a timber-framed grooved post and board wall standing on groundsills. In its new position the room was extended by the addition of a kitchen and a pantry. Two parts of the kitchen wall were built of logs, using the grooved post and board method and the rest including the pantry, were timber-framed on groundsills, with wattle infill. To this building of three partitions a stable of stone was added in the 1930s.

When taking down the house, the opening through a smoke flue was also found, and the size of the oven could be established (Ill. 46). Under the flooring broken pieces

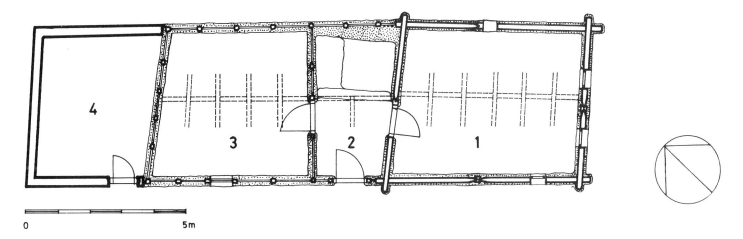

Ground plan of the Nyíri house (at the time of dismantling)

of glazed tiles were found, corresponding to the tiled smoke flue of an oven photographed in Pusztafalu in the 1930s (Ill. 44).

The undivided barn (Ill. 51), whose movable roof enables a loaded waggon to enter, belonged to a farm which could just be called medium-sized. The barns, like the *pigsty*, had timber-framed grooved post and board walls on groundsills.

The *house* and the *stable* which is integral with the *shed* on the *Erdőhorváti* croft were, at the time of their construction (1870), typical of a middle-sized farm (Ills. 47 and 48). The walls of the dwelling house comprising a room, a kitchen and pantry, are of adobe mixed with stones. This was one of the last buildings where the oven with a *kabola* (a kind of smoke flue), stoked in the room where it stood, was retained. It will be on show in the museum. The saddle roof topping an otherwise characteristically northern Hungarian house, is an indication of influence from the Great Hungarian Plain.

Besides the stable and the shed under the same roof, a *barn* (Ill. 45) and *pigsty* from *Mogyoróska* will be located in the farmyard. Both structures have timber-framed grooved post and board walls on groundsills.

The *house* on the fourth plot has also been transplanted *from Erdőhorváti*. The stone building of four divisions was erected and inhabited by people of minor gentry status whose financial position was not a bit better than that of the prosperous peasant farmers living in the same region. When it was built its ground plan arrangement was room, kitchen, pantry and stable. The conspicuously small stable was later converted into a pantry and the original pantry was turned into a room.

The large-sized vaulted open chimney is of the same age as the house itself. When it was constructed there was no heating device under it. In this house, too, the cooking, baking, heating and lighting device of the room was the oven with smoke flue, stoked where it stood, whose back part, sunk into the stone wall, came to light when the building was taken down.

The house was once ornamented in plaster, the remains of which still could be seen on the entrance front. At the end of the 19th century the building, which had no porch until then, was given a veranda of wooden posts, although structurally it was not needed at all.

Building in stone will be demonstrated by the *barn* to be re-erected in the courtyard.

73

The domestic and farm buildings from this region, furnished and equipped, will portray the material culture and living conditions of peasants living in a territory covering nearly three counties between the rivers Ipoly and Hernád in the 18th and 19th centuries. About thirty pieces of vernacular architecture will be on view (most of them having already been transplanted), although the fact has been taken into account that in the large area referred to as Palócföld a significant network of historical groups of houses preserved *in situ* as well as regional museum buildings, have come into existence and are developing.

There has always been little ploughland in the region. Hungarians who lived here from the last years of the 9th century (when their ancestors conquered the Carpathian Basin) and the Slovak and German settlers who came later, adapted themselves to the circumstances of economic geography. Besides tilling arable land, a serf would plant grapes in hillside clearings, keep animals, make tools or pursue some other handicraft. In the 18th century the serfs and cotters remained, as a result of the burdens imposed upon them by secular and ecclesiastical landlords and of the inevitable lack of production for the market, at the level of subsistence farming in joint families, and stayed within the confines of a patriarchal way of life and production.

From this social and economic status only the communities who could enforce their patent of nobility and the market towns could emerge. By the end of the 18th century the rural population of northern Hungary lived under very poor conditions, in less favourable circumstances than the greater part of the country.

Most of the region was left untouched by the capitalist development of the 19th century, though in some places efforts were made to utilize the productive capacity of the poor soils by specialization (fruit, cabbage, potato). The enactment of the law abolishing serfdom could not actually solve the economic problems of northern Hungary. In the last quarter of the 19th century many farms were made unviable by the attack of the phylloxera disease.

In the museum village we have salvaged the very last cultural historical relics of wooden architecture preserving medieval traditions and of the way of life on the „plots of clan" *(hadas telek)* of clans based on the blood ties of more than one family.

In the 18th–19th centuries in northern Hungary domestic and farm buildings were, in the majority of cases, erected in rows on the narrow crofts, running uphill at a right angle to a brook or road. At the end of the farmyard corn barns, or threshing barns with outside loading places stood parallel to the street. In the museum we have tried to represent the divisions of the structure of settlement so that wooden, timber-framed, and stone houses are represented in line with their statistical occurrence in the region. The various ways of using the fields, meadows and forests belonging to a village are shown by the structures and equipment from both inside and outside the village. The living conditions of serfs holding a unit of land under villeinage and of their descendants are also reflected by the changes in heating devices and the objects of everyday use, from home-made ones to factory-made products.

On the first croft of the one-sided street in the museum an undivided house is reconstructed on the basis of a model in *Somoskő*. The *dwelling house from Parádóhuta* is cob-walled and was erected around 1850. The building and its unceiled entrance passage *(pitvar)* has an oven, stoked where it stands, and a collar roof covered with sheaves of thatch. Smoke escaped through the triangular wattled upper part of the half hip. The pantry was added at the turn of the century. A stable with partly cob and partly adobe walls and an open shed stand opposite the farmhouse.

The first *domestic building* on the clan's croft *(hadas telek)* has come from *Márianosztra*. The pantry and the pigsty were added to the room and the passage, after 1920. The first part, the original dwelling house, was made of round timbers with cross-headed joints around 1840. The hipped collar roof was covered by stepped thatching.

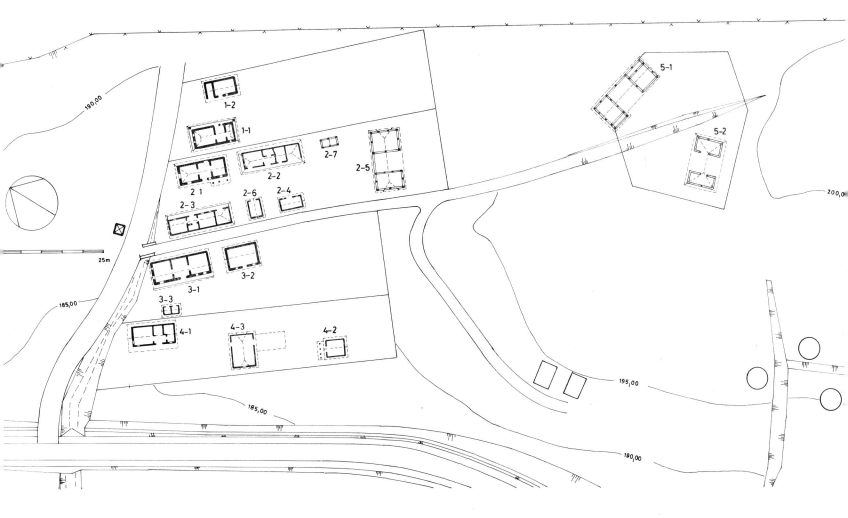

Master plan for the regional unit representing Northern Hungary
1–1: dwelling house from Parádóhuta; 1–2: stable from Parádóhuta; 2–1: dwelling house from Márianosztra; 2–2: dwelling house from Domaháza; 2–3: dwelling house from Karancskeszi; 2–4: granary from Karancskeszi; 2–5: barn from Karancsberény; 2–6: stable from Karancskeszi; 2–7: pigsty from Karancsberény; 3–1: dwelling house from Novaj; 3–2: stable from Novaj; 3–3: pigsty from Sirok; 4–1: dwelling house from Bükkaranyos; 4–2: granary from Tornaszentandrás; 4–3: oil mill from Csobád; 5–1: barn from Mikófalva; 5–2: barn from Szögliget; 6: belfry from Debercsény

There is one window in the street-front wall, and in the kitchen an asymmetrical chimney *(féloldalas szabad kémény, kémény füstölővel)* provided a vent for the smoke from the brick oven with which it forms one single unit.

The *dwelling house from Domaháza* (Ill. 53) which follows behind the Márianosztra one the "clan's plot" *(hadas telek)* comprises room, kitchen and stable with a shed added later. Here the living conditions of a poorer branch of the clan will be shown at the time of the First World War. The joint family of more than one generation lived on a few holds of land and kept two horses or cows. Grooved post and board, timber-framed log walls of the oak building are topped by a hipped collar roof with overhanging eaves. The ceiling of hewn planks rests on thirteen joists. The roof is covered with rye-straw.

Although the house was built of the materials from a demolished bigger building of grooved post and log around 1908, it can be considered a representative specimen of the northern type of farmhouse as regards its techniques of construction, its heating device and the archaic forms of use to which the dwelling place was put. The only source of heat is the "six loaves" oven of adobe bricks in the room where it was also stoked. In front of the mouth of the oven (Ill. 56), which occupies a quarter of the room, there is a ledge for an open fire, with a truncated pyramid-shaped flue of wattle-and-daub above to channel smoke into the spark catcher set up in the loft, where bacon and sausages were preserved. In the room there was also a backless bench on oak posts sunk into the earth floor under the windows looking onto the street, and on the left of the door stood a wrought iron clothes-rack. The unheated passage will be furnished as a pantry and the stable will house a trough and wooden floor for a cow and another for a horse.

The dwelling house from *Karancskeszi*, erected by the descendant of a cotter in 1883 (Ill. 54) will be put up again in the row of buildings on the right side of the clan's croft, forming a right angle with the street. The timber-framed grooved post and board walls have an infill of planks and adobe. The ceiling of boards is topped by a collar roof covered by plain tiles. The shorter front walls taper away in a thatched overhang. The house comprises a room, ceilingless passage *(pitvar)*, kitchen, pantry and pigsty. The open chimney was made of adobe and burnt bricks; in the room the stove of flat tiles, stoked from outside, will be re-erected.

The three dwelling houses will be followed by five farm buildings. The narrow back of the shoelace croft will be occupied by the large three-part *barn*, the grooved post and log walls of which were raised around 1870, to be transplanted from *Karancsberény*.

Behind the domestic building from Karancskeszi there will be a *granary* of the same provenance, holding a three-part wooden container *(hambár)* of grooved post and log walls. The *draw well*, which was constructed at the end of the last century in *Szögliget* had a rim of logs with cross-headed joints and was lined with cobbles.

In some of the villages situated on the southern slopes of the mountains Börzsöny, Mátra and Bükk, quarrying, stone-carving and masonry gained importance in the later half of the 18th century. Not only the walls of domestic buildings but also moulded window-frames, chimney copings, the mouths of ovens, the ledges in the passages,

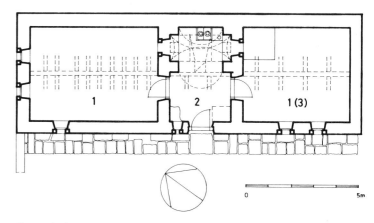

Ground plan of the Novaj house

pavements, the lips of wells, troughs, etc, were all made of dressed stones quarried in Novaj or Szomolya.

The three-partition *dwelling house from Novaj* was built in 1846 by the local mayor, a serf living on a unit of land held under villeinage. The building, which had stone foundations, was heated by two large earthenware, stack-shaped ovens stoked from the passage, which will be re-constructed. The ceiling was covered with a thick carpet of daubed reeds, and the saddle roof with collared rafters had been covered by sheaves of thatch up to 1919. The group of buildings on the croft are completed by a fodder barn *(takarmányos)* with a *stable* set up later than the house and by a *pigsty and sweep-pole well* opposite to it.

The *domestic building* on the fourth plot has been trans-planted from *Bükkaranyos*. The house, of room, kitchen, pantry arrangement, was erected without a foundation, by a serf living on a unit of land held under villeinage in 1803 (Ills. 58, 59 and 61). Originally it only had two divisions, but the pantry, too, was made of wattle; one end of the vertical stakes was sunk into the ground and their upper ends were fitted into the holes drilled in the head beam. The simple door (and window-frames of hews beams *(ács-tokos nyílászárók)* of the structure without groundsills are of the same age as the walls, with the exception of the two windows of the street front which had originally been smaller. The ridge pole roof, supported by Y-shaped uprights visible from outside, was covered by sheaves of thatch which were fastened to the laths by withes. At the time of dismantling, a stack-shaped oven, stoked from outside, heated the house (Ill. 60). Excavations revealed, however, that there had been two earlier ovens. The framed, open chimney, with wattle walls which rested on the main beam and head beam, occupied the whole place between the kitchen and the passage *(pitvar alja)*. In the second half of the last century the heated pantry was also used as a room.

For the Bükkaranyos croft, an *oil mill from Csobád* is also programmed. Sunflower seed had an increasing impor-tance in lighting, fodder, and as an ingredient in melas at Lent in the later half of the 19th century. As the oil mills owned by the community or the manor could not meet the increased demand, some farmers pressed the seeds produced in the street or part of the village for payment in the small mills set up on their crofts. The equipment, of historical engineering interest, operated in a one-roomed adobe building between 1881 and 1950.

The *granary (gabonás kamra) from Tornaszentandrás* will be located at the back of the plot. It was used to store grain and flour, but also smoked meat, vegetables, potato, turnips for cattle, wine and brandy. The reason for the preservation and display of the undivided two-storey storage chamber above a cellar is that in its timberwork a false arch of dovetail joints, a joist ceiling, survives. As tradition has it, it was set up after the fire in 1874. In the storage chamber, with simple door posts of hewn timbers, we found a three-partitioned container for grain *(hombár)*, a bread rack and a tool-stand.

On the left side of the street with four crofts, a belfry will be re-erected. The *belfry from Debercsény* is a structure of historical interest, a characteristic Roman Catholic sacral building from the 18th century. Its ground plan is square, and the walls of rustic masonry bedded in mud are unplas-tered. The oak belfry and its roof were held together by a frame of four posts. On the inner side of the stone walls, two beams held the bell, which had been cast in Vác. The

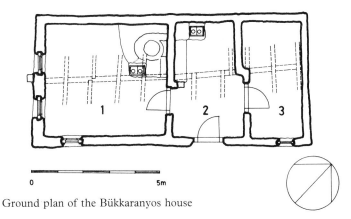

Ground plan of the Bükkaranyos house

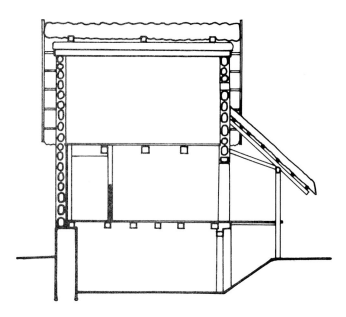

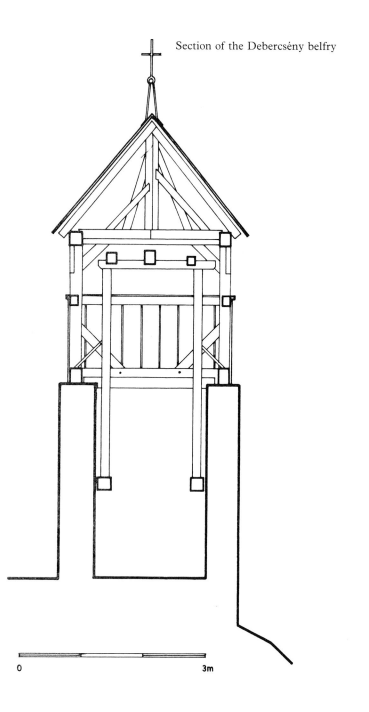

Section of the Debercsény belfry

Ground plan and longitudinal section of the Tornaszentandrás granary

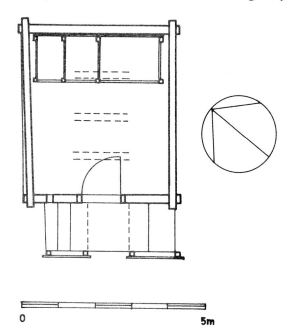

0   5m

0   3m

78

side of the structure was made of deal and the roof had earlier been covered by wooden shingles.

The carriage-road leading from beside the Bükkaranyos croft will connect the village with the outsteadings and seasonally occupied premises. First comes the outsteading called a *csűröskert* (a garden with a barn). The *barn*, set up around 1880 in *Mikófalva*, is a timber-framed building of unplastered wattle walls standing on rubble foundations and topped by a thatched saddle roof. By the threshing floor there is a place for storing hay *(szénatároló)*, a natural branch for drying grain and a bay for the chaff. At the turn of the century a shed *(rekesz)* of wattle and daub was added to the barn to serve as a sheep pen for the winter. The two-part *barn from Szögliget* with a threshing floor through which a waggon could pass was built around 1860, of barked logs. Walling is in the grooved post and log technique, with double grooved corner posts and central posts (Ill. 57). The ledged door of one of the parts has a so-called *makkos zár* ("acorn lock") whose wooden tumblers can be turned by a wooden key. The hipped saddle roof with collared rafters, is covered with stepped rye-thatch.

The path winding from the outsteading to the forest will lead to the *sheep keeping abodes (juhtartó szállás)*. This was where the sheep of a joint family of more than one generation *(nagycsalád)* grazed and slept in the summer. The group of structures—sheep-fold (karám, a [temporarily] fenced area for the day), sheep-pen (akol, a roofed construction for the night) and shepherd's hut—will be reconstructed on the basis of surveys conducted in *Váraszó* and *Szentdomonkos*.

From the shepherds' abodes, the forest path leads on to the *lime kiln* in the Bükk (beech) Mountains. On the left side of the path the *kiln* of a *Bélapátfalva* lime-burner working in a company of six *(társasba égető)* at the turn of the century will be reconstructed. By the place where the team worked in fortnightly spells, the lime-burners'

huts stand. One is a *round hut* made of laths leaning against each other to form a cone, and fixed by piling earth around them at the bottom. An open hearth laid of stones sits in the middle. The other hut "sits on the ground"; its saddle roof with ridge pole is supported by Y-shaped uprights and is covered by hewn planks.

Another important forest occupation of the 19th century will be presented in the *shingle-maker's hut* planned to be set up on the right side of the path. The structure was made of hewn laths, on the basis of a survey in *Répáshuta*. There is room for four workers under the "borogatott tetejű" roof supported by Y-shaped uprights and covered with roughly hewn planks.

The museum master plan also includes the reconstruction, based on the results of archaeological excavations, of the three-kiln *glass works* as it used to operate in *Mátraszentimre* in the 18th century. The *charcoal kiln* of Sirok will also be re-erected in the state it was in at the end of the 19th century.

The last group of buildings in the regional unit will be two *press-houses* each with a *pit cellar (lyukpince)*. The technical level of grape-growing and wine-making will be shown here as it developed on the small farms in the 19th century. Obtaining must by treading the grape was replaced by the use of the press, and instead of storing wine in a storage chamber in the farmyard, a pit cellar, built or cut out of solid rock, with a stable temperature, was constructed on the vineyard slopes. The earth-walled *press house from Nagyréde* is topped by a shingle roof covered by reeds fastened to the battens with withes. It contains a "middle-screw" *(középorsós)* wine-press. The storage cellar whose barrel vault was laid of brick opens from the earth floor. The other *press-house* transplanted from *Emőd* is cob-walled and its hip-roof is covered in reeds. It also contains a "middle-screw" wine-press, an open hearth with a fire ledge and a cauldron-stand. Wine was stored in the vaulted cellar dug into the hillside.

A chain of market towns depending on grapegrowing and trading took shape in more than one place within the Carpathian Basin as early as the 14th century and continued to flourish from the 16th century on in the central range of highland mountains. During the period of the Turkish occupation of Hungary it was these market towns which received and then sent forth the oppidan (14th–19th century market or country town) population and acted as mediators between the Great Hungarian Plain and Northern Hungary.

These highland boroughs had their privileges, which had been wrested from secular and ecclesiastical landlords and were confirmed in the 16th and 17th centuries. They also had their own market areas and did their best to utilize their town councils, adapting themselves to the order of administration of nobleman dominated and peasant counties, to serve their interests. The number of these market towns exceeded eighty as early as the 18th–19th centuries, and they carried out those central functions through which they could reach the Central European level of production for the market. Their guilds and farms were specialized, they were able to commute their feudal services for payment in money, and they were also, to a certain extent, secular and ecclesiastical centres. They grew grapes or had grapes grown on the southern slopes of the foothills of the mountain ranges of Tokaj, Bükk and Mátra and treated the wine in conformity with European commercial specifications. The red and white wines of good quality, properly filtered and aged at constant temperatures in the pit cellars, sold well and made famous these little towns in the 18th and 19th centuries.

Though small in terms of the number of inhabitants, they were important because one fifth of the population was made up of craftsmen working in guilds. For this reason, they had rights which, independently of the original social position of the town-dweller (serf, cotter or burgher), ensured for each an oppidan's rank. This gave them a degree of moral and financial safety which made them different from the surrounding serfs' villages and which, even after administrative regulations had demoted most of them into villages in 1876, expressed the burgher's consciousness and high standards of their inhabitants. In the 19th century development was checked by more than one factor. The expectations of the wine market changed, guilds as the form of organization for all handicrafts reached a point of crisis, the burdens of the fee simple absolute indemnity paid to former owner of real property in the course of land reform (manumission compensation = ? örökváltság) lay heavy on people's shoulders, and then, on top of everything, came the phylloxera attack.

The cotters, hired workers or hoers who cultivated the vineyards stood on the lowest rung of the social ladder in a market town. Next in line came the oppidan whose legal status might be cotter or serf, and who in his smaller or bigger vineyard could rise above the level of mere self-sufficiency, and usually pursued some handicraft during the winter. The small group of market town traders embraced quite a wide range of wholesalers of wine also selling their merchandise to the local grocer in foreign countries like Bohemia, Poland or Russia. Finally, there were the noble vineyard owners who did not live in the town permanently but left their mark on it in the form of mansions, cellars and tithe houses.

Master plan for the regional unit representing the highland market towns 1–1: dwelling house from Tokaj; 1–2: stone parapet and gate; 2–1: dwelling house from Tokaj; 2–2: fence and gate; 3–1: dwelling house with cellar and outbuildings from Hejce; 3–2: well from Hejce; 3–3: fence and gate from Hejce; 4–1: dwelling house from Erdőbénye; 4–2: gate and fence; 5–1: dwelling house from Mád; 5–3: well from Mád; 5–4: gateway; 6–1: dwelling house from Gyöngyös; 6–2: gateway from Gyöngyös; 7–1: dwelling house from Gyöngyös; 7–2: gate giving on the street; 7–3: gate opening on alley; 7–4: well from Gyöngyös; 7–5: stone well enclosing a Gyöngyös plot ("kőkerítés"); 8–1: dwelling house from Mád; 8–2: stone wall and gate from Mád; 9: tithe house from Mád; 10: pit cellars with walled front; 11: well from a public square; 12: stone statue of the patron saint of vineyards

The architecture of all these social groups however, shows many similarities as regards both building materials and techniques. These similarities resulted from the increasingly general practice of building in stone and from the flexible ground plan arrangement of the structures. In one of the 18th century types the upper storey comprised the room and kitchen with the press-house or cellar house and a pit cellar beneath. The upper part could later be augmented with pantry, store-rooms or workshops in accordance with the needs of the different proprietors: merchants, craftsmen or wine-growers. By the middle of the 19th century some of them developed into elongated houses (whose divisions followed one another in line) on the shoelace plots. It is a version of this type which is called Hussite house by several authors, though with no justification. What actually happened was that people associated the hillside structures with cellar-houses and the deep cellars of fortress character (dug into the hill, and vaulted) constructed in the 17th century, making use of experience gained in the erection of forts, with the Hussite wars of the 15th century. Town houses with a cellar and room for grape processing and the storage of wine, built in the 14th and 15th centuries, were identified by recent research in Sopron and Buda. It can reasonably be supposed that this medieval type of building had a renascence in the 18th century in Upper Northern Hungary, where it flourished then with the help of the carpenters' and masons' guilds. It followed the models of contemporary designs originally made by engineers or builders for structures to be raised on some large estate, utilizing the experience of earlier vernacular stone architecture and retaining the marks of historical styles in respect of ornamentation.

It is possible that in some of the market towns of Northern Hungary the conversions of the 18th and 19th centuries conceal 16th and 17th century buildings. The attention of architectural and ethnographical research was also aroused by compactly built town districts which fell outside the scope of folk architecture but did not yet fall within the scope of architecture proper (Ill. 62).

The territory between the rivers Ipoly and Bodrog proved too narrow for both farms and settlements. As a result intensive vine-growing for the market characterized the former, and tiny plots in the central parts of the small town, the latter. These plots resulted from frequent sharing out of the units of land held under villeinage in the 18th and 19th centuries, as a result of which the back of one house almost touched the front of another. Another important source of livelihood was working in the guilds, producing wooden staved containers for producers of bulk wine for the market; heat-resisting pots, glazed and unglazed; articles of clothing made of leather, wool and textiles, etc.

Buildings were chosen for exhibition in the Museum so that they will demonstrate the changes in ground plan and function of stone houses in northern Hungary during the 18th and 19th centuries. It is important to note that these domestic houses with wine house, cellar and workshop, were erected on tiny plots in overcrowded central districts without outsteadings. Direct historical contacts with 15th century (Gothic), and 18th century (Baroque) urban dwelling houses can be traced, but the execution of these buildings is simpler and they also reflect, in compliance with local characteristics and expectations, the practice of stone architecture in the villages.

We have chosen a road fork with a small triangular square forming right angles with the shoelace plots as the unit of settlement structure in the Museum. This streetscape will be completed with the supplementary elements of advanced stone architecture, like pavements, buttresses, fences and wells.

By the group of buildings typifying a highland market town we also plan to show an area of terraced vineyard slopes where the methods of cultivation and the grape varieties prevailing before the phylloxera attack can be shown.

Approaching the market town square from the left the visitor will see two *houses* that have been transferred from *Tokaj*. One is built of rubble and quarried stone. The upper storey comprises a room and a kitchen (the large-size room was partitioned into two at the turn of the century). The presshouse and workshop on the lower storey will serve in the museum for demonstrating wood turning and the preparation of shingles.

The other *Tokaj* building belonged to guildsmen. The house, in which rooms followed each other in line, was built of stone quarried in Bodrogkeresztúr early in the 19th century. The upper storey consisted of a large-sized room whose street front wall did not run parallel with the back wall. This created an acute and a blunt angle with the side walls. It had a partitioned-off kitchen and a pantry with a separate entrance (which served from time to time as the apprentice's room). The lower storey was occupied by a workshop with a timbered ceiling made of fir logs; from the workshop opened the pit cellar where wine was stored. The hipped rafter and collar roof were originally covered with wooden shingles. In the workshop, in conformity with its original character, cooper's and wheelwright's tools will be exhibited.

The *dwelling house from Hejce* was erected at the beginning of the 18th century. On the upper floor a large room and a vaulted kitchen with open chimney as well as a barn can be found. From the kitchen, stairs lead down into the press-house. The barn accommodated a cart, had room for threshing by hand and hay, too, was kept here. The barrel vaulted press-house whose entrance opened to the street was also used from time to time as a wine shop. This is the point from which, through a vaulted staircase, the deep rock-hewn storage cellar is reached. The room of the stone-walled house was heated by a flat oven stoked from outside, and in the kitchen the traces of an oven with a fire bench sited centrally were found. The owner of the house was György Petránszki, a serf living on a quarter of a land held under villeinage (1849) who had "a second class house". In addition to an eight butt piece of arable (*nyolcköblös szántó* [one *köböl* = 800 *négyszögöl*; 1 *négyszögöl* = 3.57 cubic m = 38.32 square foot]) and a five hoe (*öt kapás* [1 kapa = 200 *négyszögöl*]) vineyard, he also had a milk cow, a three-year old steer and an "old swine".

The left side of the square will be closed by the L-shaped *domestic building* to be transplanted from Erdőbénye. There are a living room and a guest room on the front of the upper floor followed by a kitchen with open chimney and the stoke holes of the ovens heating the rooms. Behind the back room of the dwelling house, built of local stone around 1770, the pantry, wine-house, stable and cart shed, added in about 1860 or so, can be seen. The lower storey is occupied by a barrel-vaulted press-house and tavern from which a storage cellar of several branches opens. The house will be furnished to reflect the living conditions of a serf who lived in a market town in the middle of the 19th century and owned a small vineyard. The pantry will house the tools of the local stone-dressing trade.

The two-storey two-unit *merchant house from Mád* was built of local stone bedded in mud. Behind the street front of the L-shaped building a shop, a room and a kitchen follow in sequence under vaults. After two rooms with planked ceiling, come the back kitchen and barrel-vaulted pantry. In the middle of the lower storey is a press-house (wine house with an open heating device also suitable for making spirits), halved by a wall plaster. On the right there are cross-vaulted store rooms and on the left barrel-vaulted wine cellars. Under the open chimney of each kitchen there is an oven with a fire bench sited centrally (*középpadka*) and from here the stoke holes of the stoves heating the rooms also open. The dwelling house, erected around 1770, has a saddle roof and collared rafters covered with tiles; the back part was added in 1860. The stone-framed doors and windows of the building, with their iron-plated shutters, testify to the skill and high standards of the craftsmen who made them.

Inside the house (Ill. 65) an attempt will be made to reconstruct an authentic late 18th century interior of hardwood furniture (a bed, a cradle, a table and chairs, etc.).

The L-shaped *dwelling house from Gyöngyös* occupied all of the shoelace plot on which it was erected. There is a cellar beneath the street front which can be entered through an arched, keystoned, stone-framed gate. The house was made of local stone bedded in mud at the end of the 18th century, and its back part, looking onto the

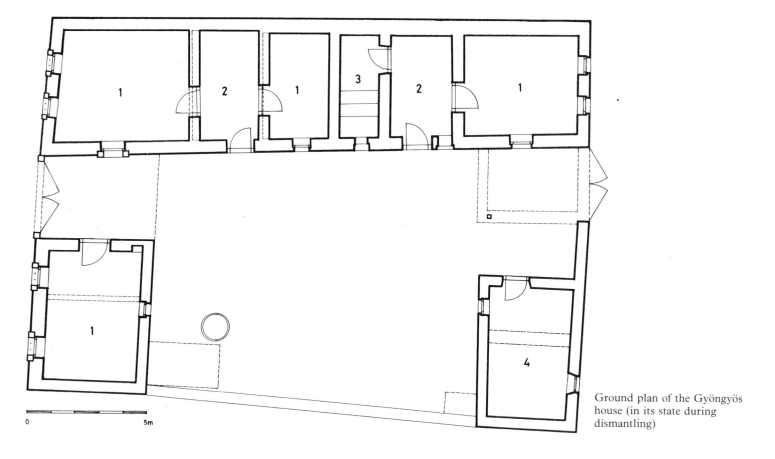

Ground plan of the Gyöngyös house (in its state during dismantling)

courtyard, was added around 1850. The doors and windows are stone-framed. In the middle of the façade there is a niche. The two rooms of the street front were heated by stoves of flat tiles stoked from under the eaves *(eresz-alj)*. The saddle roof with collared rafters over the planked ceiling was covered with tiles. The two dwelling units were connected by a stretch of farm buildings consisting of a privy, a shed and a stable.

The house, erected on a unit of land which had originally been held under villeinage and belonged to the estate of Baron Orczy, was used by a viticulturist burgher family.

The second and third units were let to a hoer and to a craftsman and his family. The house will be furnished accordingly.

The next *dwelling house,* taken down in *Gyöngyös,* was built around 1820 (Ill. 66) on a plot which lay between two alley-ways and could be crossed by a waggon. The U-shaped two-unit building *(zárt építésű)* was made of local Farkasmály stone by a joint family of more than one generation having the legal status of cotters, who lived on grape-growing and cartage. On the southern side of the croft there is an arched gate in a stone frame flanked by two

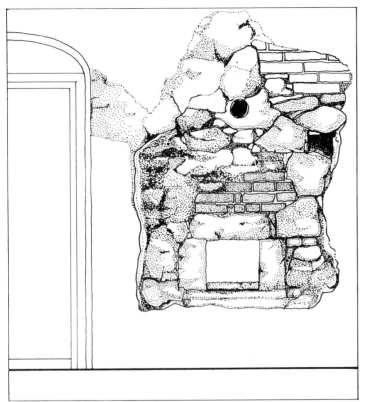
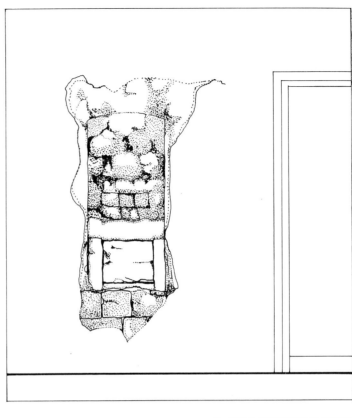

Detail of the oven in the Gyöngyös house at the time of dismantling (first room)

0   1m

windows on each side. On the left a room, kitchen, room, pantry, then another kitchen and room follow in line, with a brick-vaulted cellar beneath which is accessible from the courtyard through the steps under the pantry. On the right side of the plot, the street front consists of a room ("the old people's home"), with a stable behind, which also served as a winehouse from time to time. The saddle roof with collared rafters was originally covered by shingles of wood. From under the open chimney of the first kitchen the "eyed" green stove in the front room, and the stack-

shaped oven of plastered wattle and daub in the back room, were also stoked, according to information given at the time of dismantling. The furniture will give a comprehensive view of the wide range of products turned out by the local guilds in the 1870s.

The *dwelling house from Mád*, whose divisions follow in line, was built in the first years of the 19th century. The building, consisting of room, kitchen, room and pantry arrangement topped by a hipped saddle roof covered with tiles, is the last in the tiny square in the museum. The

85

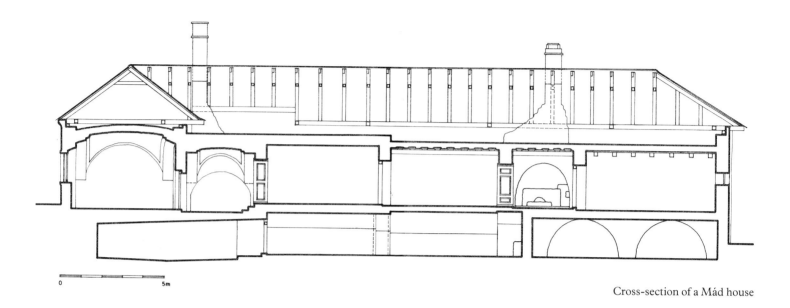

Cross-section of a Mád house

rectangular oven, stoked from under the open chimney in the kitchen, heats the room and is under floor level. (Descriptions of similar heating devices can be found in excavation reports on 16th century villages). The family of vinegrowers (descendants of cotters), added to their house in about 1870 a separate vaulted pit cellar. The croft is surrounded by a fence of stones bedded in mud.

According to the museum master plan the *tithe house from Mád* will be re-erected (Ill. 63) by the road leading to the terraced vineyards. The three-storey stone building, which was built early in the 18th century, served for the storage of wheat and wine submitted by the serfs to their landlords as tithes. In front of the terraces of the hill under vineyards (Ill. 64), a *stone statue* of the vinegrower's patron saint, *Donat* (made in Gyöngyös, 1759), will stand.

The museum unit representing the market towns of Upper Hungary is completed by the *Greek Catholic church* (Plate XXX) transplanted from *Mándok* which used to belong to Szabolcs County. The building, which is of outstanding historical importance, was built of oak

logs and covered with fir wood shingles in 1670. This is the oldest wooden example of vernacular architecture in Hungary. According to historical data, it was Hungarian families belonging to the United Greek Church and immigrants from Carpatho-Ukraine, who arranged for the construction of the small affiliated church with its divided nave, whose sanctuary has a straight end, and which includes a belfry.

When re-erecting it in the museum several necessary reconstructions had to be made, to restore the church to the state it was in when newly erected. These included re-erecting the wall structure with a door dividing the nave, the iconostasis separating the sanctuary from the nave and re-roofing with a collared roof construction of long rafters coming a long way down *(csüngőszarufás)*.

From the original furniture of the church, whose façade is neither plastered nor whitewashed, we have managed to preserve the 18th century bell, the richly carved and painted royal door *(királyi ajtó)*, the altar-leg and a few sacral objects. Objects as authentic as possible from the points of view of history, liturgy and ethnography, necessary for completing the furniture of the church, have been ensured with the assistance of other museums and the Greek Catholic Churches. The icon wall of the church is adorned with three late 18th-century rows of painted icons. Also to be found here are the dated pinewood sitting furniture, the processional flags and the icon-holding stand. (Plate XXXI). The cemetery surrounding the church has been reconstructed on the basis of direct analogies and wooden graveposts have been set up there, transferred from the neighbourhood of Mándok. With the timber-framed mortuary the group is now complete.

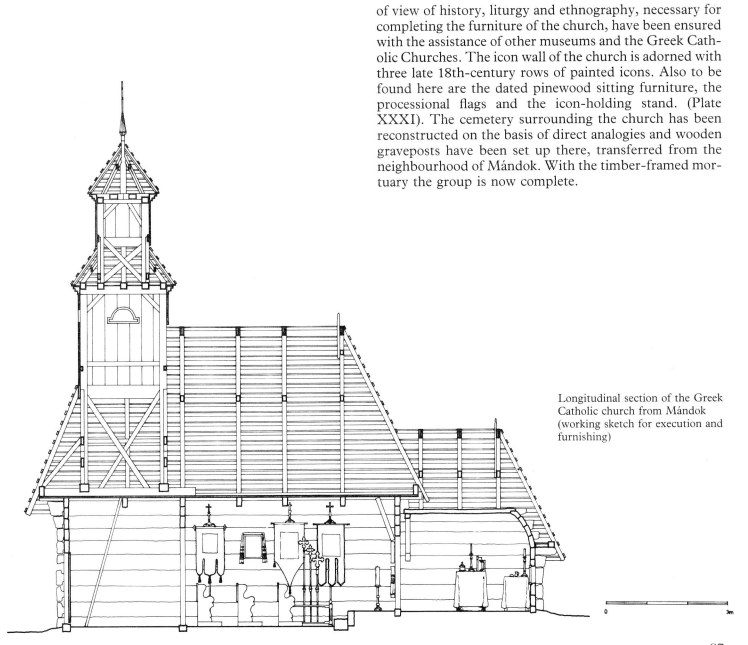

Longitudinal section of the Greek Catholic church from Mándok (working sketch for execution and furnishing)

0   3m

SELECTED BIBLIOGRAPHY

A detailed survey is given of open air ethnographic museums and of regional museum houses preserved in situ in: Albert KURUCZ–Iván M. BALASSA–Péter KECSKÉS (ed): *Szabadtéri néprajzi múzeumok Magyarországon* [Open Air Ethnographic Museums in Hungary]. Budapest, 1987, p. 180, with 226 pictures. A bibliography covering earlier special literature is that by Zoltán KOVÁCS: Szabadtéri néprajzi múzeumok [Open Air Ethnographic Museums]. *Index Ethnographicus XI.* Budapest, 1966, p. 146. A comprehensive review with references of the European material relating to this type of museum, is given in: Adelhart ZIPPELIUS (red): *Handbuch der europäischen Freilichtmuseen.* Köln, 1974, p. 272. There is also a bilingual (German/English) edition of the report on the Conference of the Association of European Open Air Museums held in Szentendre: Claus AHRENS–Iván M. BALASSA–Adelhart ZIPPELIUS (red): *Tagungsbericht Ungarn 1982 Report of the Conference 1982.* Szentendre, 1984, p. 226.

The most recent summaries concerning Hungarian folk architecture and interior decoration are: Jenő BARABÁS–Nándor GILYÉN: *Magyar népi építészet* [Hungarian Vernacular Architecture]. Budapest, 1987, p. 204; Iván M. BALASSA: *A parasztház évszázadai (A magyar lakóház középkori fejlődésének vázlata)* [Centuries of the Hungarian Peasant House (A Draft Outline of the Development of Hungarian Dwelling Houses in the Middle Ages)]. Békéscsaba, 1985, p. 191; Klára K. CSILLÉRY: *A magyar népi lakáskultúra kialakulásának kezdetei* [The Beginnings of Interior Decoration in Hungarian Vernacular Buildings]. Budapest, 1982, p. 390.

Definitions of the special expressions, objects and structures occurring in the book can be found in: Gyula ORTUTAY (chief ed.): *Magyar Néprajzi Lexikon* [The Encyclopaedia of Hungarian Ethnography]. Vol. I–V, Budapest, 1977–82.

General summaries in German and English: Iván BALASSA–Gyula ORTUTAY: *Ungarische Volkskunde.* Budapest–München, 1982, p. 870. Iván BALASSA–Gyula ORTUTAY: *Hungarian Ethnography and Folklore.* Budapest, 1984, p. 820. Tamás HOFER–Edit FÉL: *Ungarische Volkskunst.* Budapest, 1981, p. 638; Tamás HOFER–Edit FÉL: *Hungarian Folk Art.* Budapest, 1979, p. 638.

The two series of the Szentendre Village Ethnographic Museum, complete with summaries in German: the yearbooks *Ház és Ember* [House and Man], (ed. Péter KECSKÉS) and the informative periodical *Téka* (ed. Györgyi H. CSUKÁS) have appeared since 1980.

Some sources concerning the buildings, ways of life, history of science and exhibitions covered by this book:

BALASSA, M. Iván:
A Néprajzi Falu az Ezredéves Kiállításon [The Ethnographic Village at the Millenary Exhibition]. *Ethnographia*, LXXXIII, 1972, pp. 553–72.
Dél-Borsod település- és építéstörténetének vázlata (A Szabadtéri Néprajzi Múzeum Közép-Tiszavidék tájegysége/ [An Outline of the History of Settlement and Architecture in Southern Borsod (The Area Representing the Central Tisza Region in the Open Air Ethnographic Museum)]. *Ház és Ember 1.* Szentendre, 1980, pp. 111–50.
Szentendre, Freilichtmuseum IV. Die reformierte Kirche aus Mánd und der Glockenturm aus Nemesborzova. Budapest, 1987, p. 16.

BALÁZS, György:
Szentendre, Freilichtmuseum I. Ober-Theiss-Gebiet. Budapest, 1983, p. 16.

BARABÁS, Jenő–SZOLNOKY, Lajos:
A Szabadtéri Néprajzi Múzeum tudományos tervének váz-

lata [An Outline of the Scientific Plan for the Open Air Ethnographic Museum] (mimeographed manuscript). Budapest, 1967, p. 31.

BÍRÓ, Friderika
Az Őrség ház- és lakáskultúrája a 18. század végétől napjainkig [Vernacular Architecture and Interior Decoration in the Őrség from the End of the 18th Century to Our Days]. Szombathely, 1975, p. 275. Zala és Vas megye paraszti ház- és lakáskultúrája a 19. században. (A Szabadtéri Néprajzi Múzeum Nyugat-Dunántúl tájegysége) [Peasant Architecture and Interior Decoration in Zala and Vas Counties in the 19th Century (The Regional Unit Representing Western Transdanubia in the Open Air Ethnographic Museum)]. *Ház és Ember 1.* Szentendre, 1980, pp. 53–77.
Göcsej. Budapest, 1988, p. 298.

BÍRÓ, Ibolya:
Szentendre Freilichtmuseum III. Die kleine ungarische Tiefebene Budapest, 1987, p. 16.

BOROSS, Marietta:
Kovácsműhely Szilsárkányról [A Smithy from Szilsárkány]. *Néprajzi Értesítő LVI.* 1974, pp. 105–19.

K. CSILLÉRY, Klára:
Das Freilichtmuseum in Szentendre. *Cibinium 1974–1978.* Sibiu, 1979, pp. 415–31.
A Szabadtéri Néprajzi Múzeum kialakulásának előtörténete [A Prehistory of the Formation of the Open Air Ethnographic Museum]. *Ház és Ember 1.* Szentendre, 1980, pp. 9–33.
A szabadtéri múzeumok berendezési problémái [The Problems of Furnishing Open Air Museums]. *Ház és Ember 2.* Szentendre, 1984, pp. 153–61.
Statisztikai vizsgálatok a magyar népi bútorok történetéhez [Statistical Research into the History of Hungarian Vernacular Furniture). *Ház és Ember 3.* Szentendre, 1985, pp. 183–200.

H. CSUKÁS, Györgyi:
A Bakony és a Balaton-felvidék népi építészete (A Szabadtéri Néprajzi Múzeum Közép-Dunántúl tájegysége) [Vernacular Architecture in the Bakony and the Balatonfelvidék (The Regional Unit Representing Central Transdanubia in the Open Air Ethnographic Museum)]. *Ház és Ember 2.* Szentendre, 1984, pp. 21–61. Asztalosok Szentkirályszabadján [Joiners at Szentkirályszabadja]. *Ház és Ember 4.* Szentendre, 1987, pp. 113–136.

FLÓRIÁN, Mária:
Épületkiválasztástól a bemutatásig (Az uszkai kisnemesi ház példáján) [From Choosing a Building to its Presentation (Demonstrated by the Minor Gentry's House in Uszka)]. Szentendre, *Téka, 1983,* Nos. 2–3, pp. 1–58.
Ober-Theiss Region. *Regionale Baugruppen im Ungarischen Freilichtmuseum 1.* Szentendre, 1987, p. 82. A debercsényi harangláb [The Belfry in Debercsény]. *Ház és Ember 4.* Szentendre, 1987, pp. 103–12.

GILYÉN, Nándor–MENDELE, Ferenc–TÓTH, János:
A Felső-Tiszavidék népi építészete [Vernacular Architecture in the Upper Tisza Region]. Budapest, 1975, p. 215.

GRÁFIK, Imre:
A makói paraszt-polgár ház [The Peasant-Burgher's House in Makó). *Ház és Ember 1.* Szentendre, 1980, pp. 157–74.
A Szabadtéri Néprajzi Múzeum "alföldi mezőváros" tájegysége (A 18–19. századi alföldi mezővárosi fejlődés kérdéséhez) [The Regional Unit Representing a Market Town in the Great Hungarian Plain in the Open Air Ethnographic Museum] (On the Question of the Development of Market Towns in the Great Hungarian Plain in the 18–19th Centuries)]. *Ház és Ember 4.* Szentendre, 1987, pp. 7–42.

HOFFMANN, Tamás (ed.):
A Szabadtéri Néprajzi Múzeum (Szentendre) telepítési terve és épületjegyzéke (Master Plan and List of Buildings

for the Open Air Ethnographic Museum, Szentendre] (Mimeographed manuscript). Budapest, 1970, p. 129. *Néprajz és feudalizmus* [Ethnography and feudalism]. Budapest, 1975, p. 234.

JANOVICH, István:
A szabadtérbe kihelyezett fatárgyak hiánypótlása fa felhasználása nélkül [Completing Incomplete Wooden Objects Placed in the Open, Without Using Wood]. *Ház és Ember 2.* Szentendre, 1984, pp. 251–262.

KÁLDY, Mária:
Élő múzeum (A Szabadtéri Néprajzi Múzeum közművelődési munkájáról) [A Living Museum (On the Public Educational Activities in the Open Air Ethnographic Museum)]. *Téka, 1985,* No. 1, pp. 2–25.

KECSKÉS, Péter:
A Szabadtéri Néprajzi Múzeum tudományos előkészítése és telepítési terve [Scientific Preparations and Master Plan for the Open Air Ethnographic Museum]. *Ház és Ember 1.* Szentendre, 1980, pp. 35–50. *Szentendre, Freilichtmuseum II.* Die griechischkatholische Kirche aus Mándok. Budapest, 1983, p. 16. Egy letenyei présházpince felmérése és áttelepítése [Survey and Transplantation of a Press House Cellar from Letenye]. *Ház és Ember 3.* Szentendre, 1985, pp. 173–82.

KOVÁCS, Judit:
A Szabadtéri Néprajzi Múzeum 1982. évi látogatottságának vizsgálata [A study of the attendance at the Open Air Ethnographic Museum in 1982]. *Ház és Ember 4.* Szentendre, 1987. pp. 175–86.

RASSY, Tibor:
A Szabadtéri Néprajzi Múzeum Történeti Adatgyűjteménye [The collection of Historical Data in the Open Air Ethnographic Museum]. *Ház és Ember 2.* Szentendre, 1984, pp. 221–49.

SABJÁN, Tibor:
Adatok a kályhásmesterségről I. (Völcsey Lajos, Dör) [Data Concerning the Stove-Tile Makers' Trade (Lajos Völcsey, Dör)]. *Ház és Ember 4.* Szentendre, 1987, pp. 134–57.

VARGHA, László:
Eredetiség és rekonstrukció a Szabadtéri Néprajzi Múzeumban [Authenticity and Reconstruction in the Open Air Ethnographic Museum). *Ház és Ember 2.* Szentendre, 1984, pp. 123–36.

ZENTAI, Tünde:
A dél-dunántúli település és építkezés változásai a 19. században (A Szabadtéri Néprajzi Múzeum Dél-Dunántúl tájegysége) [The Changes in Settlement Pattern and Architecture in Southern Transdanubia in the 19th century (The Regional Unit Representing Southern Transdanubia in the Open Air Ethnographic Museum)]. *Ház és Ember 1.* Szentendre, 1980, pp. 79–109. Az őcsényi ház bontása [Dismantling the House in Őcsény). *Ház és Ember 2.* Szentendre, 1984, pp. 175–202. (Made jointly with Tibor SABJÁN).

THE PROVENANCE OF THE HOUSES AND COMMUNAL BUILDINGS IN THE OPEN AIR ETHNOGRAPHIC MUSEUM

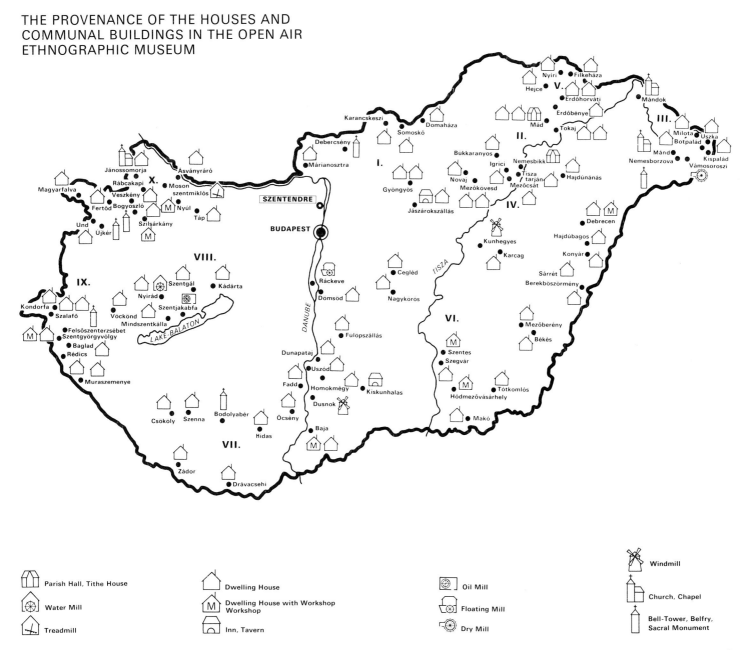

Parish Hall, Tithe House

Water Mill

Treadmill

Dwelling House

Dwelling House with Workshop
Workshop

Inn, Tavern

Oil Mill

Floating Mill

Dry Mill

Windmill

Church, Chapel

Bell-Tower, Belfry,
Sacral Monument

MASTER PLAN OF THE OPEN AIR ETHNOGRAPHIC MUSEUM

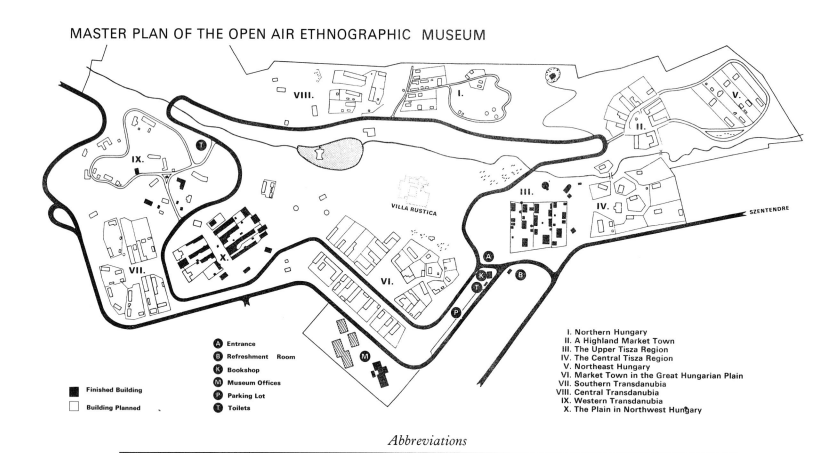

VILLA RUSTICA

SZENTENDRE

A Entrance
B Refreshment Room
K Bookshop
M Museum Offices
P Parking Lot
T Toilets

I. Northern Hungary
II. A Highland Market Town
III. The Upper Tisza Region
IV. The Central Tisza Region
V. Northeast Hungary
VI. Market Town in the Great Hungarian Plain
VII. Southern Transdanubia
VIII. Central Transdanubia
IX. Western Transdanubia
X. The Plain in Northwest Hungary

■ Finished Building
□ Building Planned

Abbreviations

1 room	(front, back, living, bed and anteroom)
2 kitchen	(passage, permanent place for cooking and/or baking)
3 pantry	(storage chamber for food, utensils or grain)
4 stable	(stable, cow-house, sheep-pen)
5 pen	(pigpen and hen-house)
6 barn	(outhouse for the storage of threshed and unthreshed corn, etc.)
7 workshop	(potter's, carpenter's, furrier's, cooper's, etc. workshop)
8 press-house	(place for grape processing)
9 cellar	(place for storing wine or produce)
10 shed	(shed, cart-shed)
11 veranda	(on the street front or on the courtyard side of the house)

1 Fireplace in the Mezőtarpa house (S. Ébner)

2 Interior of the barn from Tiszabecs (J. Szabó)

3 The structure of the walls of the Kispalád house (Z. Erdélyi)

4 Hay barn with moveable roof ("abora") from Tiszabecs (J. Szabó)

5 The sheep-pen from Botpalád (J. Szabó)

6 The wood-shed from Kispalád (J. Szabó)

7 The belfry
from Nemesborzova
during re-building
(I. Janovich)

8 The Csire-zug in Mezőcsát, a relic of an agglomerated settlement (J. Szerencsés)

9 The Nemesbikk parish hall (I. M. Balassa)

10 Agglomeration of houses in the centre of Mezőkövesd with an example of a special thatch overhang at the gable (Zs. Bátky)

11 The house from Igric (I. M. Balassa)

12 The house from Tiszatarján (M. Gáspár)

13 The protruding entrance, with windbreak walls from Mezőkövesd (I. M. Balassa)

14 Chaff holder from Mezőkövesd (I. M. Balassa)

15 Porch of the Mezőcsát house (J. Szerencsés)

16 The Mezőcsát stable-with-fireplace, having a protruding entrance with windbreak walls (I. M. Balassa)

17 The porch of the
Mezőkövesd house
(J. Szabó)

18 Street front of the Szegvár dwelling house (I. Gráfik)

19 Porch of the Karcag house (I. Gráfik)

20 A dresser from Debrecen (J. Szerencsés)

21 Street front
of the Tótkomlós house
(J. Szabó)

22 Maize holder of basketwork in Letenye (Zs. Csalog)

23 Fence of cleft piles with a gate having a bottom bar ("szántalpas kapu") (I. Kovács)

24 The dwelling house from Csököly (T. Zentai)

25 The Muraszemenye house (Z. Erdélyi)

26 View of street in Szentgál (S. Gönyei)

27 Dwelling house from Mindszentkálla (Gy. H. Csukás)

28 Entrance front of the Nyirád water mill
(J. Szabó)

29 Pair of crushing
stones in the
Szentjakabfa oil-mill
(Z. Erdélyi)

30 Millstones and hopper of the Nyirád water mill
(J. Szabó)

31 Dwelling house in Szentgyörgyvölgy (I. M. Balassa)

32 Street front of the Vöckönd house (I. M. Balassa)

33 Barn with protruding threshing front and entrance in Iklódbördöce
(I. M. Balassa)

34 The Szalafő house enclosing its courtyard (I. M. Balassa)

35 Part of the farmyard enclosed by the Szalafő house (I. M. Balassa)

36 Street with houses making a herringbone pattern ("fűrészfogas beépítésű utca") in Agyagosszergény (S. Gönyei)

37 Left side streetscape of the regional unit representing the plain in North-Western Hungary in the Museum (P. Deim)

38 The right side of the street in the Museum (J. Szerencsés)

39 Manorial wine-press from Nyúl, 1699 (M. Gáspár)

40 Kitchen interior in the Süttör house (J. Szerencsés)

42 Stone statue of St. John of Nepomuk from Csepreg, late 18th century (J. Szerencsés)

41 The Mosonszentjános votive chapel (1842) in its original place (M. Gáspár)

43 In the Mosonszentmiklós tread-mill (P. Deim)

44 Tile oven with smoke vent on its left in a Pusztafalu dwelling house (S. Gönyei)

45 The barn in Mogyoróska (J. Szerencsés)

46 The Nyíri dwelling house during dismantling
(I. M. Balassa)

47 Stable and shed in Erdőhorváti (I. M. Balassa)

48 Dwelling house in Erdőhorváti (I. M. Balassa)

49 Hay barn in Kovácsvágás (J. Szerencsés)

50 Polygonal barn in Füzérradvány (J. Szabó)

51 Barn with one storage bay ("egyfiókos csűr") in Nyiri (I. M. Balassa)

52 Fruit-drier in Pusztafalu (S. Gönyei)

53 Dwelling house in Domaháza (B. Molnár)

54 Street front of the Karancskeszi house (J. Szabó)

55 Picket-fence in Szögliget (P. Kecskés)

56 Oven stoked in the room in which it stands in the Domaháza house
(P. Kecskés)

57 The barn in Szögliget during dismantling (P. Kecskés)

58 Under the eaves of the Bükkaranyos house (P. Kecskés)

59 The trussing and walling of the Bükkaranyos house during dismantling (P. Kecskés)

60 Oven in the room of the Bükkaranyos house (J. Szabó)

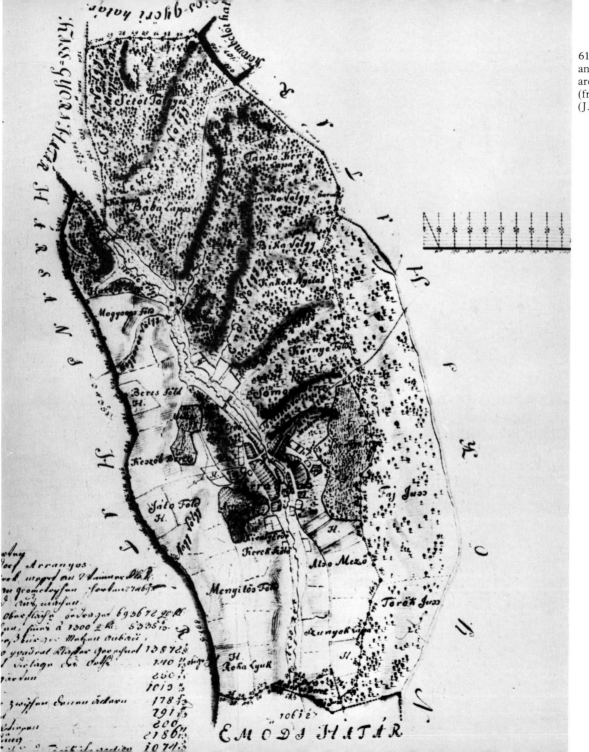

61 Bükkaranyos
and surrounding fields
around 1770
(from the OL Kneidinger map)
(J. Szabó)

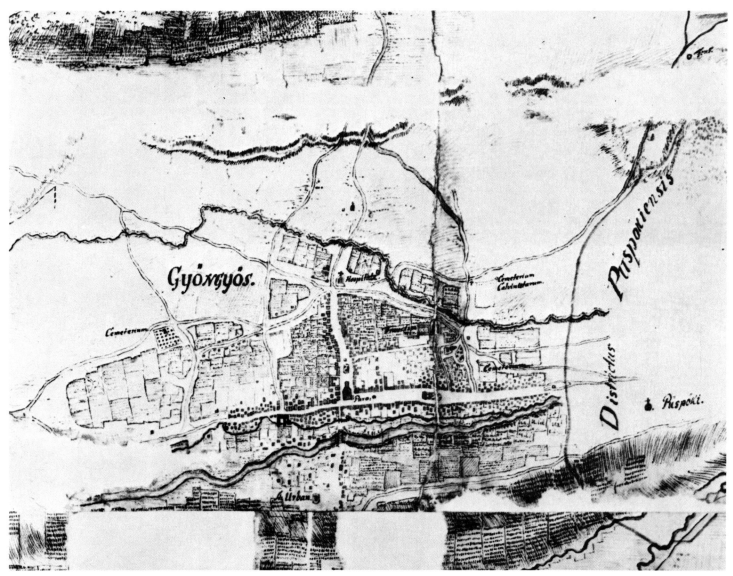

62 The settlement structure of Gyöngyös around 1750 (National Archives)

63 The tithe cellar in Mád
(second half of the 18th century) (P. Kecskés)

64 Stone revetments on the vineyard-clad hills at Mád (P. Kecskés)

65 Bed and cradle from the furniture of the front (best)
room of the house in Mád (J. Szerencsés)

66 Street front of the Gyöngyös dwelling house
(Zalka M. u. 30.) (P. Kecskés)

I View of village in museum unit representing the Upper Tisza region (L. Szelényi)

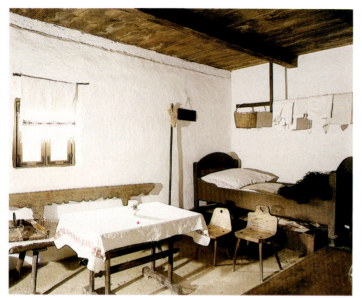

II Furniture in the back room of the Botpalád dwelling house
(J. Szerencsés)

III Pigsty on the Botpalád croft (J. Szerencsés)

IV "Almárium" or wardrobe in the front (best) room of the Botpalád
house (J. Szerencsés)

V Interior of the back room of the Uszka house
(J. Szerencsés)

VI The room where visitors to the Uszka
house were received (J. Szerencsés)

VII Stable and dwelling house on the petty noble's croft (J. Szabó)

VIII View of street with the Protestant church from Mánd
and the belfry from Nemesborzova (L. Szelényi)

IX Interior of the Protestant church from Mánd (L. Szelényi)

X The dry mill from Vámosoroszi (J. Szabó)

XI The wooden graveposts from Szatmárcseke (J. Szerencsés)

XII Street front of the Mezőkövesd house (J. Szerencsés)

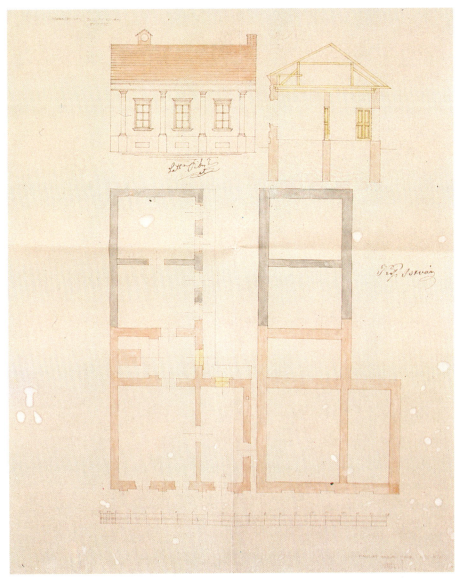

XIII Coloured technical drawing of the Debrecen house (J. Szerencsés)

XIV The Drávapalkonya house as seen from the courtyard (J. Szerencsés)

XV Painted chest from Komárom (lst half of the 19th century) from the furniture of the Kádárta house (J. Szerencsés)

XVI Inlaid chest (1830) from the furniture of the Szentgál house (J. Szerencsés)

XVII The Szentgyörgyvölgy house in the museum (J. Szerencsés)

XVIII Interior in the first room of the Magyarfalva house (J. Szerencsés)

XIX The kitchen in the Magyarfalva house (J. Szerencsés)

XX Right side of the street in the regional unit representing the plain in North-Western Hungary in the Museum (M. Gáspár)

XXI Interior of the first room in the Jánossomorja house (J. Szerencsés)

XXII Interior of the front (best) room in the Bogyoszló house
(J. Szerencsés)

XXIII The kitchen in the Bogyoszló house (J. Szerencsés)

XXIV The main beam in the back room of the Bogyoszló house
(J. Szerencsés)

XXV Painted footboard of a bed from the furniture of the Süttör
house (J. Szerencsés)

XXVI The kitchen in the Táp house (P. Deim)

XXVII Füzérradvány
(J. Szerencsés)

XXVIII The Pusztafalu apiary
(J. Szerencsés)

XXIX A dwelling house in Filkeháza
(I. M. Balassa)

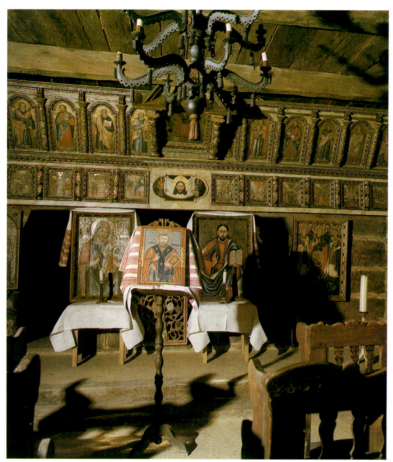

XXX Inside the Greek Catholic Church from Mándok (J. Szerencsés)

XXXI The Greek Catholic Church from Mándok in the Museum
(J. Szerencsés)